THE ANYWHERE
OPERATING SYSTEM

The Anywhere Operating System

How to lead a team and run your business from anywhere

LUKE THOMAS

Aisha Samake

Friday Feedback, Inc

CONTENTS

PREFACE

Hey there! I'm Luke Thomas, the founder of Friday. I want to kick things off by sharing why I wrote this book.

My story (2013-2019)

My experience working remotely started almost a decade ago. At the time, I was a recent college graduate who moved to Boston, Massachusetts, in search of finding an "interesting" job in technology, but my wife and I planned on leaving as soon as we could. I knew that living in Boston was a temporary home and the only way I could leave was if I could take my job with me. I wasn't willing to move to another location (especially somewhere more rural) if I wasn't able to work on interesting things.

Six months after the move to Boston, I started working remotely as a contractor for a startup based in Silicon Valley. At the same time, 37 Signals (now known as Basecamp) released a book called: *Remote*. This book shaped my thinking and reinforced what I felt. If I work from a laptop, and my laptop can go anywhere, why do I need to live in Boston? Why can't I relocate to a place where I want to live and still do meaningful work?

I discovered that working from anywhere had a lot of promise, *but it also wasn't easy*. At times, I felt lonely working out of my tiny apartment. Some days I didn't know what I was supposed to work on. I didn't really know my coworkers or my boss well, either.

Despite the challenges, I couldn't shake the feeling I had working from that 500 square-foot apartment. The freedom and autonomy was addicting. I felt like I was living in the future.

As my career advanced, I worked for a few different distributed companies in a variety of roles (individual contributor, team leader, executive) and was able to move out of Boston a few years ahead of schedule with my wife, who could also work remotely.

We ended up moving to Portland, Maine, and noticed an instant improvement to our quality of life. We didn't have to spend two hours a day commuting, we lived closer to family, and were in a place that we *wanted* to be. Work no longer dictated where we lived.

At the time, I worked for a startup based in Nashville, Tennessee, and we would travel down and spend winters there, escaping the snow and cold in the Northeast. The entire time, we would regularly ask ourselves, "Is this real life?"

But working remotely still felt way too tough.

At every distributed company I worked for, I would repeatedly run into the same problems. It was difficult to answer questions like:

- What are people working on?
- Why does my work matter? How does it fit into the bigger picture?
- Who are my coworkers? Are they people or robots?
- Why am I spending my day sitting in boring meetings?

This itch drove me to start Friday (the company, not the day). I saw a need in the market and wanted to explore ways to help.

When things started to get interesting (2018-present)

I worked on Friday as a side hustle for a while, growing the idea enough to discover that there was an opportunity worth pursuing. I quit my day job in September 2019, raised a small amount of funding, and was able to hire a few engineers to explore possible solutions.

At the time, there was a growing number of companies (especially early-stage startups) that were struggling to hire in cities like San Francisco, New York, and Boston, so they were increasingly building distributed teams out of necessity.

Working on my startup accelerated the pace of learning. I was able to see what other companies were doing, but I also had the opportunity to share the lessons I learned after working remotely for several years. We could also take the lessons learned and build software to help.

At the time, about 2% of the US population was working remotely. Many investors were curious about this nascent market, but it wasn't large enough back then. Remote work was a nice-to-have, but not a must-have for most organizations.

Then COVID-19 hit.

Approximately 10 times as many people are working fully remote now. Organizations are cutting back on office space. Numerous companies have shifted their operations to a work-from-anywhere model. Most research indicates that most companies will adopt a hybrid approach moving forward.

The way we work has changed.

2020 completely changed the face of work. As a result, many of you are trying to chart a new path into the unknown.

Why I wrote this book

I wrote this book because I couldn't find a practical how-to guide on how to run a business and lead a company from anywhere. Existing books are too theoretical and not actionable enough. After COVID, many of you don't need to be convinced that working from anywhere is the future. What you want to know is how to make this new approach *actually* work.

I've spent almost a decade working remotely. I've learned many important lessons from our customers. I've see what works and what doesn't. I've also spent a ton of time reading through decades of research on how to work on distributed teams.

At the end of the day, I concluded, *"why don't I just write the book I wish I had."* And here we are!

About the co-author, Aisha.

I'd like to introduce you to Aisha Samake, my co-author for this book. Aisha has been working at Friday as a content marketing intern from Northeastern University for the past few months, and has written her own books in the past. I thought it would be useful to have her share her perspective, especially as she's new to working from anywhere.

Aisha was working part time at her university when COVID hit, and she had to quickly shift from working in an office to working from home, while navigating online classes. Throughout the book, Aisha will share an employee perspective on the topics covered so we can unpack the advice from a variety of angles.

A quick aside before we jump in

If you have feedback or would like to chat about the topics in this book, please ping me:

- **Email:** luke@friday.app
- **Text:** (629) 240-2263

You can read the online version of this book and access a free audio book (plus other downloadable content) at: **www.friday.app/anywhere**

I

THE FOUNDATION

THE HIGH-LEVEL BUILDING
BLOCKS AND FOUNDATIONAL
PRINCIPLES YOU NEED TO KNOW.

| 1 |

What if the office is the new invention?

Let's establish the foundation of this book by outlining the history of the office and from where it came. It's important to ask the question: "Is working from anywhere a new idea or are we returning to a way of working that was normal in the past?"

What if the idea of going into a busy city center to a dedicated workspace is new compared to working from anywhere? Perhaps history can provide clues into what the future holds?

Where did the office originate?

The idea or the use of the word "office" started in ancient Rome. The Romans had a business district at the center of their town, with shops, offices, and government bureaus. The Roman word "officium" loosely means "bureau," which gives us the word "office" that we use so often today.

In the 15th century, we see evidence of monks who worked in a place called a scriptorium. This was an office-like environment where monks would work in small cubicles. Scritoriums were places where they could write, work, and do deep thinking.

In the 18th century, the office started to gain meaningful traction. The East India Company presents a clear example of a purpose-built office, which is currently known as the Ripley building. This structure was created to handle complex bureaucracy and trading between Europe and Asia. Charles Lamb, a novelist, documented his time working in this building and reported on environment. They would work from 10 A.M. to 11 P.M! Workers were granted perks like holidays and bonuses, but there also were downsides that Lamb mentioned. For example, he wrote,

> "You don't know how wearisome it is to breathe the air of four pent walls without release day after day."

Sounds like a great time, right? Let's keep going.

The UK government referred to an office environment in the following way:

> "For intellectual work, separate rooms are necessary. So that a person who works with his head may not be interrupted, but for the more mechanical work, the working in concert of a number of clerks in the same room they're proper superintendents is the proper mode of meeting it."

The basic idea is that people who work with their mind shouldn't be interrupted, so a separate room was necessary. On the other hand, for mechanical work it was important that everyone be in the same room to make supervision easy for managers. It also was easy to do administrative work and store written records and books when the work happened in one place.

In the 19th century, we saw the invention of the light bulb. This innovation encouraged people to work longer hours. Before this, people had to use candles and literally burn the midnight oil.

In the 20th century, we see the the office explode in popularity. Urbanization was driving the rise of cities, and the idea of the open office floor plan started to take shape. Frank Lloyd Wright is a well-known architect who inspired this floor plan to be developed down line. It had fewer walls, with a bullpen environment that resembles the open-office floor plans of today.

As the floor plan advanced, so did the technological improvements. Electric lighting, telegraphs, telephones, typewriters, calculators, etc., were all developed. Then you saw the growth of skyscrapers. We saw the growth of scientific management by Winslow Taylor, which was focused on quantifying every aspect of work. In 1939, the Johnson Wax Company had an open-office floor plan that brought bright lights, warm spaces, and cork ceilings to the office space.

In the 1960s, the action office was invented by Robert Propst, which allowed for more privacy for certain workers. This led the way for the rise of the cubicle, which allowed organizations to easily adapt their floor plans.

As we navigate history, there's a clear trend that emerges. The office was a way of coordinating a group of people with its roots deep in manual work. With the rise of technology, the internet, and the ability to communicate with coworkers across the world at a moment's notice, perhaps it is time to rethink if the office makes sense for the world we live in today?

Maybe the work-from-anywhere movement is grounded in thousands of years of history, whereas the office is the new invention? When we frame it this way, it makes the idea of not going into an office everyday feel a bit more normal.

The final point I'd like to make is that as you'll learn in the remainder of this book, we are not against working in an office. The shift and the beliefs that we have about the way work is moving is that people work in a variety of ways. As a business, if you want to build a highly productive and engaged workforce, you will need to offer each employee a choice.

For some, that may be going into an office every day of the week. For others, it may be working two or three days a week from home and then going into the office to meet up with coworkers. Some people may want to be fully remote and live in the middle of nowhere.

In a world where each person has flexibility and autonomy, the office can no longer be relied on to create the structure, connective tissue, and collision space for your team to get work done. If this is a permanent shift, you will need to rethink how you communicate, operate, and lead.

But is this a permanent shift?

Work from
anywhere

The Workplace

| 2 |

Is working from anywhere a fad?

Major movements in society arrive like waves crashing on the beach. For the work-from-anywhere (WFA) movement, the wave was like a tsunami when COVID-19 arrived in early 2020. Our world changed overnight.

A huge wave is formed by a variety of factors – Wind. Underwater disturbances. Volcanic eruptions. Earthquakes. Similarly, the work-from-anywhere wave has several contributors too.

If we want to understand if the WFA shift is sustainable and truly the "future of work," we need to dig beneath the surface and try to find what is causing the wave. That's what the remainder of the chapter is about.

Don't bet against network effects

The most important thing you should think about, as you plan for this new future of work, is to recognize that WFA has network-effect-like characteristics. For those unfamiliar with network effects, it's a phenomenon where the strength of a product or movement strengthens *as more people join.*

For example, Facebook was not valuable when there were 100 students using it at Harvard. The Facebook network is much stronger and much more valuable with billions of people around the world using the platform.

We can see a similar dynamic at play with remote work. According to the Buffer State of Remote Work survey, 97% of respondents said that they would like to continue working remotely (at least some of the time).

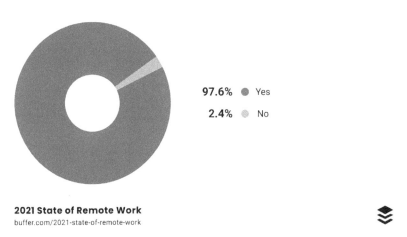

Would you like to work remotely, at least some of the time, for the rest of your career?

97.6% ● Yes

2.4% ○ No

2021 State of Remote Work
buffer.com/2021-state-of-remote-work

Additionally, 97% of respondents would recommend remote work to others. Put simply, the people who experience this way of working don't want to go back *and* they overwhelmingly recommend it to others.

As a leader, what are the implications here?

If you don't adopt this new way of working, *your hiring pool will get smaller over time* as more people join the work-from-anywhere network. Some of your best employees will leave and go work for competitor who offers flexibility. Does this make you nervous?

The COVID-19 pandemic accelerated an existing shift

As you already know, the COVID-19 pandemic forced the desk-bound population to work from home for over a year. It can be difficult to separate the signal from the noise. Is this a permanent shift or a short-term impact from COVID? We're going to examine what was happening before the COVID-19 pandemic started and see if these factors are still in motion today.

Another contributing factor is that you were probably already working in a distributed way before the pandemic. If you worked with coworkers in other offices, you were already working in a distributed way, but you could rely on the office to fill in the gaps and help you connect with your team.

What is creating the wave?

Now that we've mentioned the high-level principles, let's get into the specific factors that accelerated the rise of distributed work.

1. Specialized talent & geographical constraints

The first factor is that people with specialized skills are in high demand, especially in major metros. There's only so many people with a particular skill set in a given city.

This means that companies had a limited supply of candidates within driving distance from the office, which forced them to look elsewhere. At this point, the company has a couple options:

1. Recruit from away, and convince them to move closer to the office
2. Recruit from away and let them work-from-anywhere

It's much easier to recruit if you give candidates a choice instead of forcing them to move. This is especially true if the potential hire has a spouse who works, a family, and roots in their community. It's one thing to move as an individual; it's another to move as a family.

Additionally, someone with a specialized skillset has leverage during negotiations. If the company is desperate enough to make a hire and a great candidate doesn't want to move, the candidate can vote with their feet by not taking the job.

Before the COVID-19 pandemic, we saw this happen quite a bit with technical talent. I have no reason to believe this trend won't continue after the pandemic subsides.

2. The rising cost of living

Before the COVID-19 pandemic, the cost of living soared in major cities, with no real increase in the value that was being provided to the residents. You paid for the same unit of housing, yet the price would continue to rise.

Take a look at the cost of a one-bedroom apartment in major cities around the United States before the pandemic hit:

- San Francisco - $3,546/mo median rent
- New York - $3,073/mo median rent
- Boston - $2,595/mo median rent

While it's reasonable to expect people will still live in the city, it's also fair to assume that some percentage of people would rather live elsewhere, with a dedicated home office, more space, and cheaper housing.

Are you are willing to skip over talented people who don't want to live near your office?

3. The commute

Another factor that drove the early growth of remote work was the increasing amount of time spent commuting. The average commute in the US was 27 minutes (one way). Since 2010, that number has grown by 2 minutes. While this doesn't sound like a lot, the reality is that people were spending almost an hour a day doing something that they probably didn't want to do. I remember when I lived in Boston, I would spend at least an hour a day squashed alongside people on the local subway. I hated it. It felt like an epic waste of time.

While there's no problem with driving, listening to podcasts, and decompressing at the end of the work day, you might want to do something else, like hang out with your kids or friends. Maybe you decide to use the extra free time to learn a new skill or pursue a hobby?

As the pandemic subsides, I think it's safe to assume that forcing a commute will be frowned upon. While some travel is fair, being forced to travel every day is a different story.

4. Millennials are growing up

Another contributor to the wave of working from anywhere is the reality that the largest group in the US labor force is millennials. What do we know about millennials? They are getting married later.

Why do we care? As this group settles down, they begin having kids; they may want a house in suburbia instead of a condo in the city.

Why does that matter? This matters because there's a gravitational pull toward living further outside the city by the largest part of the workforce. This means people will be spending more time commuting if we go back to the way things were before COVID.

5. The pace of technological change

Technology continues to accelerate, especially if we look at the past few years. For example, some of the most popular tools for remote work were created after 2010 (Zoom in 2011, Slack in 2013, and Microsoft Teams in 2017).

As someone who's been working on building remote work tools for years, many investors previously wrote off this category because they didn't think the market was big enough. To be fair to them, it probably wasn't. At least before 2020.

What this means for you is that we are going to see a lot of innovation over the next few years. There will be tons of remote work apps vying for your attention. Companies like Facebook will aggressively invest in virtual reality technology like Oculus to create the feeling of connection when working-from-anywhere.

6. The pioneers paved the way

In the late 2000s, forward-thinking companies paved the way and showed us how to work-from-anywhere. Basecamp and others forged a path for startups like Zapier, GitLab, InVision, and Automattic. These forward-thinking organizations have shown us that it's possible to scale a company without an office as several of them now have over 1,000 employees (and growing!).

These early leaders love to teach and share what they learn. They write books, open-source their company handbooks, and teach classes. This public content and willingness to share has reduced the risks associated with remote work for newly formed startups, which accelerates adoption.

7. The office was designed for collaboration, not deep work

Finally, we have the reality that the office was built for a particular style of work that is focused on real-time collaboration and spontaneous interactions with coworkers. The open-office floor plan is intentionally designed to encourage random collisions at the water-cooler. While this is okay in small doses, it is not conducive for doing deep, thoughtful work.

I remember when I worked at the office, I would have to put on noise-cancelling headphones to "tell" my coworkers that I was trying to get stuff done. Even then, people would tap me on the shoulder with a question, which drove me nuts. At times, I would need to ask my boss if I could leave the office to do heads-down work.

But will it stick?

Back in 2013, Yahoo ended its remote work policy and required that employees come back into the office. A reasonable question to ask is: *"is what happened in 2013 a sign of things to come?"* Is working from anywhere a short-term trend caused by COVID, or a lasting change?

My hope is that by listing out the factors that have accelerated the work-from-anywhere shift, you can come to your own conclusions. If you look at the factors causing the wave, do you expect them to grow or subside in the future? Do you expect the rate of technological change to continue or stop? Do you expect that people will opt into a commute again every day of the week or not?

If you expect this shift to continue, you should keep reading :)

| 3 |

How our environment shapes the way we communicate

At this point, I hope we've convinced you that there's a major shift underway in our world. This shift has the potential to change the way we live and work.

Now, I'd like to discuss the pain that you may feel as you adapt to this new way of working. I call this idea, "the gap." While I am a remote work advocate, it's also important to be realistic and intellectually honest instead of spouting hype. There is no perfect solution. Remote is not perfect. The office is not perfect.

If we want to navigate this change, we need to understand the benefits of remote and the strengths of the office. Then, we need to build a way to bridge the gap between the office and a work-from-anywhere model.

A day at the office

Imagine a day at the office. You walk in the front door a few minutes before 9 a.m., which creates an visual reminder that it's time to enter work mode.

You arrive at your desk, collect your thoughts, and power up your computer. You go to the kitchen and make coffee. In the kitchen, you run into a coworker from another team. You say hi and ask how their weekend went – small talk ensues. Over the course of the discussion, you discover that another department is working on a cool project that you didn't know about before.

You return to your desk, put on headphones, and start replying to emails. You scramble to do work before chaos hits. After the team shows up, you have a daily standup meeting where everyone shares what they did yesterday, what they are working on today, and any blockers they face. It's not the best use of your time, but this ritual makes you feel a bit more connected and aware of what people are working on. You go back to your desk and resume working. Your coworkers are chatting next to you, but you have noise cancelling headphones on so it doesn't bother you too much.

After a bit of work, you look up and see coworkers through the glass conference room doors in a meeting. Things look tense. Is that the finance team? Interesting. You wonder if you should ping them. Perhaps it's related to end-of-quarter results?

Lunch time arrives and you grab a bite to eat with a colleague. You chat about work, but you also shoot the breeze and find out if they have any interesting plans for the weekend.

After lunch, you try to do more heads-down work, battling emails, Slack notifications, and other pings. You go to a couple meetings and try to free up time to get things done.

A couple hours later, you wrap up your day feeling a little behind the ball, but it's time to go home. You bring your laptop. Hopefully you won't have to do too much work later after the kids go to sleep. You get stuck in traffic on the way home, so you end up arriving late and can't spend as much time with the kiddos.

Rinse and repeat. Friday can't come soon enough.

Then COVID hits.

A day working from home

Now, you're forced to work from home. Thanks, COVID-19.

Instead of walking into the office, you try to find space in your home to get things done. You create a makeshift desk at the kitchen table. Work and life happens in one place now. You power up your computer while you make coffee in the kitchen.

Within a few minutes, chaos arrives. Emails start coming in. Coworkers start pinging you on Slack at the worst possible times. Meanwhile, your kiddo has to stay home and he's not excited about spending the entire day with you.

As a leader, you decide to run your daily standups over Zoom at 9 a.m., but they feel a bit different when remote. People are tripping over each other on the call. You look at one of your coworkers and they are living the dream. They have their own home office, no frustrated children, and a big smirk on their face.

The workday continues. The pings won't stop. The meeting invites drive you nuts.

Is Bob even working? It looks like he's never online when you check Slack. Meanwhile, your coworkers are breathing down your neck. They want to schedule an update meeting. It's impossible to know if your team is working on the most important things right now. It's a freaking pandemic after all. At the office, you could walk over to where your team was congregated and ask them what they were working on. It used to be so easy. Not anymore!

You sit at the kitchen table, frustrated about the situation. You feel disconnected and out of the loop. The online communication makes you feel like your team is a bunch of emotionless robots and not the friendly people you remember from the office gatherings.

You decide to schedule a virtual happy hour with your team so you can shoot the breeze and catch up. It ends up being awkward and everyone seems tired and excited for the call to end. You miss the in-person water-cooler chats; your team is becoming demotivated and tensions are high. Miscommunication is rampant.

Despite the struggle, you see potential. If you could figure this out with your team, you could cut out the two-hour commute and get some of your life back. When the pandemic ends, the kiddo could go back to school and you could focus again. Maybe you can build out one of the bedrooms and turn it into an office. Maybe you could work from your favorite coffee shop a couple mornings a week.

You are intrigued by this way of working, but everything is so stressful right now.

How our environment shapes how we work and communicate

If you compare the office and home, the average day looks and feels quite a bit different.

When you walk into the office, you are constantly gathering data through observation and osmosis. This environment activates your senses (sight, sound, maybe even smell) to understand what's going on. Working from the office is like watching a movie in high definition. When you chat with coworkers, you can read their body language, tone of voice, and more. It's easy to pull your team into a room for a quick meeting or white-boarding session.

If you think about the design of the office (especially an open office floor plan), these spaces are intentionally built to encourage random collisions and interactions with coworkers.

While this environment is ideal for collaboration and quick conversations, it's a terrible place to do heads-down, focused work. If you want to do your best thinking, you need to put on noise-cancelling headphones.

On the other hand, when you work outside the office, it's easy to feel disconnected. You have less data that you can observe. You need to rely on your email inbox, Slack, or endless Zoom calls to understand what people are working on. If working from the office is like watching a movie in HD, working from home is like watching an old movie in black and white.

With that being said, working from home has the potential (at least when it's not a pandemic) to give you a newfound sense of freedom over your day. In theory, you can work *where* and *when* you are most productive. You can focus and do more deep work compared to the noisy office. You can take a break and go for a walk if you need to clear your mind. And there's no commute. You have more control over your time and it feels good.

The gap

When you work remotely, it's easy to feel like you are missing out...because you are! This is the gap. It's the difference between what you used to experience at the office and how you are feeling right now. You miss the context and awareness that you had at the office.

It's normal to use the existing tools in your toolbox to try to bridge this gap too. You try to replicate the office environment online with a virtual office tool. You want to feel more connected with coworkers, so you schedule a Zoom happy hour. Many of these efforts fail. What do you do?

Building a bridge to cross the gap

The good news is that there's a way to build a bridge to cross this gap, but it will require a different approach than that which you are accustomed to. You can't rely on more Zoom calls or another ping in Slack. The tools that worked well at the office don't work as well in this new world. You need a different set of tools, methods, and processes to build the bridge to cross the gap.

| 4 |

The secret that's hiding in plain sight

Let's talk about the secret to the work-from-anywhere movement that's hiding right out in the open. This secret is one of most important concepts you need to know if you want to unlock a better way to work. To kick things off, let's examine a seemingly simple statement you've heard from coworkers before:

"I love working from home!"

When a coworker says they love working from home, someone of you may instantly think, *Is this person taking crazy pills? Why do they like isolation? I need social interaction. I miss the energy of the office, and I like being around people. I can't spend every hour of the day at home.*

I've heard these statements over and over; and, as an extrovert, I get it. I like social interaction too, but this shift is not actually about being able to work from home.

If the shift to work-from-anywhere is about spending every day of the week sitting on video calls and workplace chat in a home office, I will be the first person to go back to the office.

What are the benefits to working remotely?

Why do people say they like working from home? Is this high-level statement a code-word for something else? Is there something deeper here that we need to unpack?

According to a FYI survey, people love remote work because it offers freedom, *flexibility*, no commute, and increased productivity. According to research from Buffer, the #1 benefit respondents cited was a *flexible* schedule.

I could share more research and data, but the conclusion is straightforward. People like working from home because of the flexibility it provides. It's not about sitting in your home office, disconnected from the rest of the world. It's about having autonomy and being in control of your day more than you were before.

As someone who's worked remotely for several years, I like remote work because it helps me better integrate work and life. I have more control over my time. I don't need to commute and waste an hour a day sitting in my car in rush hour traffic. Instead, I can go for a walk, learn a new hobby, or hang out with my family.

I want to drive this point home (pun intended), because it's critically important if you want to build a high-performing team or company.

High school vs. college

For those of you who graduated from high school and attended college, do you remember what the experience was like?

In high school, you had to stay at school all day. There was a butts-in-seat mentality and you had to be present all the time.

College was different. You had a lot more freedom. While you were expected to show up to class on time, when the seminar was over, you could leave and go back to your dorm and study (or play video games). I thought college was much better than high school because I had more control of my time.

Likewise, the workplace is growing up and graduating, too. Your employees are adults, not high-schoolers. They want more control over their time. They want you to trust that they will get the work done, no matter what their daily routine looks like.

For some, that may be working from home every day of the week. For others, that may be working from the office a couple days and home the rest of the week.

Is this good for business?

At this point, you may agree with me, but you may ask, *"Is this change good for the business?"* If this shift negatively impacts workplace productivity, a competitor will come along, compete against you, and win.

If implemented correctly, working from anywhere is good for the employee and the business. It's a win-win for everyone, which is rare.

To illustrate my point, look at what Peter Drucker, a famous management consultant, said in the late 1990s:

> "The most important contribution management needs to make in the 21st century is to increase the productivity of knowledge work and knowledge workers."

He then proceeded to list six major factors, one of which I've included below:

> "It demands that we impose the responsibility for their productivity on the individual workers themselves. Knowledge Workers have to manage themselves. They have to have autonomy."

The modern workplace is no longer the factory floor. In the past, if you weren't present, production would grind to a halt. Knowledge work is not a physically demanding activity. It's about what's happening in your head. Are you able to do your best thinking? Do you have enough time to do deep work without interruptions? Are you giving your team autonomy to work when they are most productive?

For example, I'm writing this chapter right now at 5 a.m. before my kids wake up. I am much more productive early in the morning instead of the afternoon. A coworker may have the opposite preference.

Everyone has different approaches when it comes to their personal productivity. Working a strict 9-5 p.m. schedule can be difficult for people who have different lifestyles and preferences. People are different. By allowing colleagues to work when they are most productive, the company as a whole can benefit.

This doesn't just happen naturally

One big disclaimer: this state of work nirvana doesn't happen automagically. It takes work, especially as a leader. Sometimes your colleagues act like they should to go back to high school. Sometimes people have trouble figuring out when they are most productive. Sometimes teams need to negotiate and meet in the middle.

Making this shift is not easy, which is why I've written this book. I want to help you reduce or eliminate the pain that I've felt over the years. I want to help you translate this big idea into action. Your employees deserve it.

In conclusion: it's more than the "where"

To wrap up: when coworkers say, "I love working from home", it's about when they work instead of only thinking about where they work from. That's the secret hiding in plain sight!

Hey guys :) Need some help with copy

10:30am

Sure thing! Send it over

10:50am

I'll give it a look too!

11:00am

Thank you!

11:00am

It's done! Green helped with some edits too

2:00pm

| 5 |

The key ingredient of WFA: Asynchronous Communication

I f the work-from-anywhere movement is about a more flexible work environment that gives the individual autonomy to decide **when** and **where** they work, we need to dig in and see what's preventing us from making this change. This transition is still in its early innings for many of you, whether you realize it or not.

Unfortunately, the modern workplace is addicted to constant presence to move work forward. It looks like never-ending Zoom calls and constant chatter in Slack. If we want to build a future-proof team or company, we need to make some changes asap.

What's hindering the work-from-home movement?

1. Habit

The first roadblock is that we are creatures of habit. The office encouraged constant collaboration and was intentionally built to maximize real-time interactions. Meetings were cheap and coordination was easy. When everyone was in the office at the same time, it was easy to find a coworker and ask them a question. Constant presence meant work was happening.

It turns out that office habits are difficult to change, especially with a group of people. It can be tough to reverse this gravitational pull as you try to make the shift to remote.

2. Unspoken expectations

The next contributor to a brittle work environment is unspoken expectations. You may be okay with the idea of a more flexible workplace for your team, but it's possible you didn't clarify and reinforce this idea enough, so your team still believes they need to be present from 9-5 p.m. People may worry that they might get into trouble if they go for a walk after lunch or finish their day a bit early to hang out with family or friends.

3. Meetings

According to Atlassian, the average employee has 61 meetings per month, with half of them considered to be a waste of time. The average middle manager spends up to 50% of their time in meetings. The average organization spends 15% of its time in meetings. If the average person spends almost one day every week in meetings, that creates a shaky foundation from the start.

While it's impossible to eliminate all your meetings at work, especially with customers and external stakeholders, it is possible to dramatically reduce the amount of time you spend in them, especially if they are poorly run and ineffective. To illustrate, consider the dreaded status update meeting:

That feeling...

4. Workplace chat

Next up, we have workplace chat software. Like meetings, workplace chat is an effective way to collaborate and coordinate work with colleagues, but it assumes that we should collaborate all the time, which reminds me of the office at its worst. Too much of a good thing can be a bad thing!

To illustrate, Microsoft conducted research at the beginning of the pandemic showing that team leaders sent 115% more messages in Microsoft Teams than before COVID hit. We also can see a steady stream of articles that outline how workplace chat is overwhelming and functions like a never-ending treadmill, keeping us distracted and unable to do deep work.

Slack, I'm Breaking Up with You

Samuel Hulick (Follow)
Feb 29, 2016 · 10 min read

Too much chat(ter)

According to RescueTime, of the time people spend working in front of a computer, 5% is spent using work chat. This software inadvertenly creates an expectation that the recipient will reply right away. After all, that's how chatting in the real world works! RescueTime research also shows that 40% of knowledge workers are unable to get 30 minutes of uninterrupted focused time in a workday because they are constantly interrupted by these tools.

That's not all. Slack and Teams also project a constant state of presence, which is the digital equivalent to someone walking around and making sure you are sitting at your desk working. If someone is away from the computer, their status will automatically mark them as offline, which reinforces the "butts-in-seat" mentality that desperately needs to be changed in a work-from-anywhere model.

The issues with workplace chat tools have prompted remote-first companies like Zapier, Automattic, Stripe, and Shopify to create their own "intranet" to encourage slower and more thoughtful communication.

This pain is why I founded Friday. I find tools like Slack to be an essential piece of the work-from-anywhere software stack, but you need rules and logic to ensure that things don't get out of hand.

Now that we understand the roadblocks in our way, let's talk about the solution. But first, let's talk about a big word that you need to know.

What is asynchronous communication?

Asynchronous communication is when two or more people communicate without the requirement that they be present at the same moment in time. For example, if I send you an email, you could read and reply *at a time that makes sense for you.* If I send you a handwritten letter in the mail, you can read it when it arrives, and reply at a time when it makes sense for you.

Asynchronous communication is a more flexible way to communicate because the sender and receiver don't need to be present at the same time.

On the flipside, if I wanted to jump on a Zoom call with you, we'd need to schedule a time where both of us can be present *at once.* If you can't make it, communication does not happen. This is synchronous communication; it is not flexible by design because it requires all parties to be present. It's a much more rigid way to communicate.

Why does asynchronous communication matter?

If you spend most of your work week in meetings or in chat (like research indicates), you have laid a foundation where the presence of others is *required* to move work forward. Every real-time conversation creates a potential blocker that will need to navigate. The more your day is spent working on someone else's time and schedule, the more inflexible and brittle your workday becomes.

Meetings as the last resort, not the first option

To be clear, I am not advocating for ditching meetings and real-time human interaction completely. Instead, I believe that you should reduce your reliance on meetings and real-time communication to get work done, saving meetings for when they are most important.

When you worked at the office, the environment encouraged synchronous communication as the default. It was easier to hold meetings. You could walk up to a coworker and start a conversation right away. It was easy to have white-boarding sessions.

Now, the coordination cost is much higher when everyone is apart. It's much more difficult to align schedules, especially with teams across time zones. As a result, it's more practical to communicate asynchronously by default.

This shift looks something like the following image.

Modes of Communication

Distributed Teams

Asynchronous	Synchronous

Colocated Teams

Synchronous	Asynchronous

In fact, the longer a company works from anywhere, the more they want to communicate asynchronously by default.

Find the balance

Now, you will need to unlearn some of the habits that the office previously encouraged. You need to find a healthy balance between real-time conversations and asynchronous communication.

Each communication method is a tool in your WFA toolbox. There's a time when it makes sense to jump on a Zoom call. There's also a time when it makes sense to share an asynchronous update using a tool like Friday.

In the next chapter, we're going to discuss the different communication tools at your disposal and when it makes sense to use them. It's easy to say that the key to working from anywhere is to communicate asynchronously, but if we want to be successful, we need to translate this high-level idea into action.

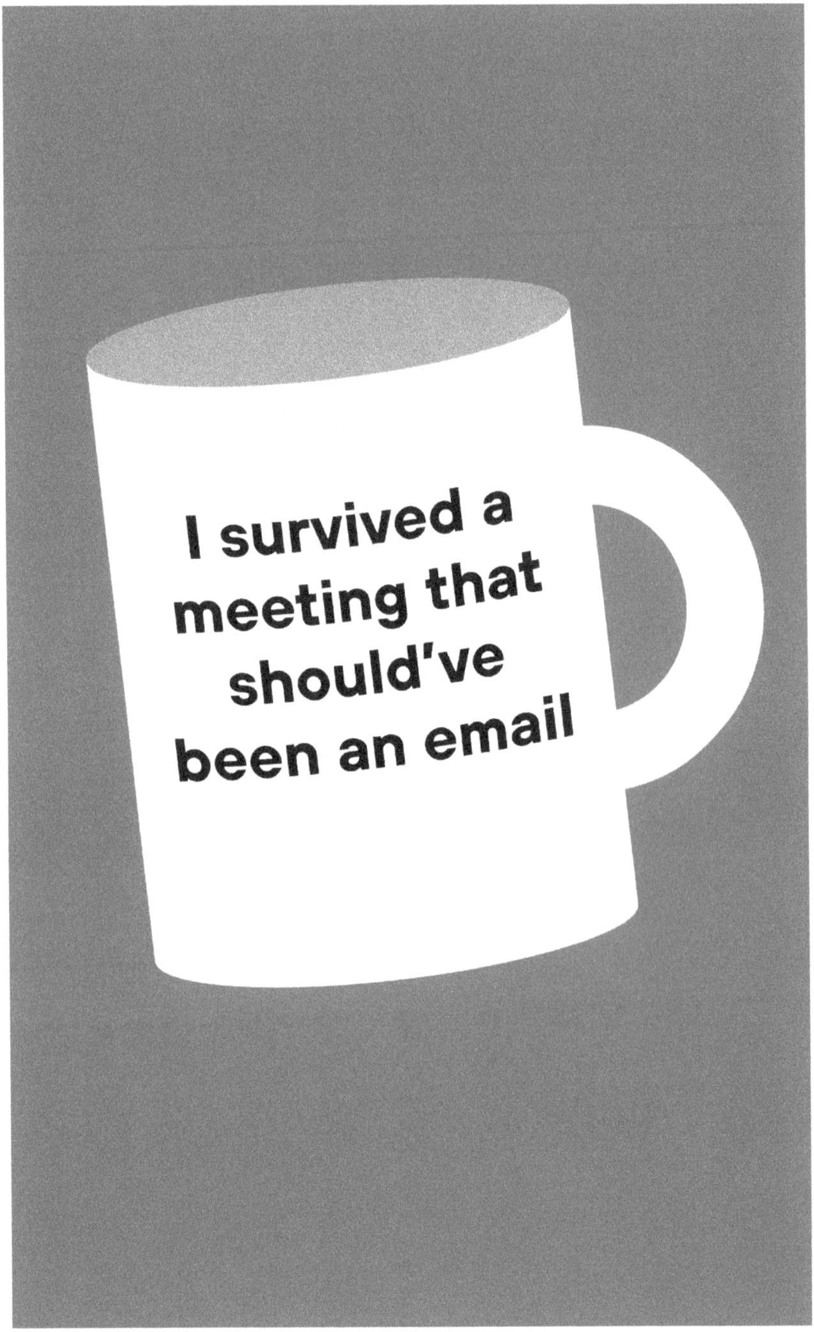
I survived a
meeting that
should've
been an email

| 6 |

That meeting should have been an email

If the key to working from anywhere is to work asynchronously by default, what should we do next? When should we share a written update instead of jumping into a Zoom call? When is asynchronous communication most appropriate?

If we want to become an expert communicator, we need to know what tools we have in our toolbox and when we should use them.

Components of Communication

At a high-level, communication can be broken down into two parts: **conveyance** and **convergence**.

Huh?

Let me explain! I promise it's worth it.

Conveyance

Conveyance is the transmission of information by the sender and the processing of that information by the recipient. If you have shared a written status update or sent an email before, you've *conveyed* information to someone else.

For the audience, the information *conveyed* provides useful context, but it takes time to read, watch, and interpret the message. You need time to turn the *conveyed* information into meaning. **When your message primarily involves conveying information, you should default to asynchronous communication.**

Convergence

Convergence is when two (or more) people negotiate and arrive at a shared understanding around a topic or an idea. The information shared in the conveyance step serves as the bedrock for *converging* and getting on the same page.

Convergence looks like it sounds. It's when people negotiate and build a shared, collective understanding, removing ambiguity along the way. **When you need to converge around a topic and build shared meaning with others, you should communicate synchronously most of the time.** You need a fast feedback loop that a real-time conversation provides to get on the same page.

Relationship Strength

You also need to consider the strength of your relationship(s) with stakeholders. If you know someone well, you've already established mutual understanding of how each other works and you can be more casual in the way you communicate. The strength of your relationship is like oil, it makes conversations run more smoothly.

What's your communication superpower?

Now that we understand the basic components of communication, we need to look at the communication tooling we have and learn more about their superpowers. Synchronous communication has some strengths, while asynchronous communication is more adept in other ways.

If we want to unlock new levels of productivity when working from anywhere, you need to know how to navigate back and forth between these modes of communication.

1. Asynchronous superpowers

When you compose a message asynchronously, you are unlocking specific superpowers that this form of communication enables. Asynchronous communication is:

- **Revisable** — you can change or edit your message to maximize clarity for the recipient
- **Persists by default** — your communication is automatically stored on a "hard drive" and can be referenced later, which helps reduce miscommunication
- **Multi-threaded** — When communicating asynchronously, it's possible to communicate with multiple people in parallel
- **More honest** — when communicating behind a screen, the person composing the message is unaware of how they might be perceived because they can't read your body language and other nonverbal cues. At times, this can lead to more unfiltered and honest communication; while, at times, it can be more composed because the person is trying to predict how you might react in advance.
- **Scalable** — Asynchronous communication can scale much better than real-time conversations because recipients have the abil-

ity to process the message at a time that makes sense to them. This is why you see live TV shows with millions of viewers, but a highlight clip on Youtube may have ten times the number of views.

2. Synchronous superpowers

Real-time communication has specific superpowers too, like:

- **A fast feedback loop** — quick, back-and-forth discussion helps you get on the same page, faster.
- **More data to interpret** — 80% of communication is conveyed through non-verbal cues, like tone and body language. The richness of this data can help accelerate relationship-building and make it easier to establish common ground. It's like watching a movie in 4k instead of a black and white video from the 1930s.
- **More immersive** — it's impossible to have multiple conversations at once. This forces focus, which can be useful when you need someone's undivided attention.

How to pick the ideal communication tool?

Unfortunately, there is no right answer that works for all scenarios because each conversation is different and can evolve quickly. With that being said, the communication method you choose has an outsized impact on the way you are perceived and understood by others.

This is why you need to become an expert at picking the ideal communication method for the job at hand. Consider the following questions:

- **Relationship strength** — how well do I know the person?
- **Clarity of conversation** — how clear or unclear is the conversation?

I've developed a 2x2 framework to help you think through when it makes sense to communicate synchronously vs. asynchronously.

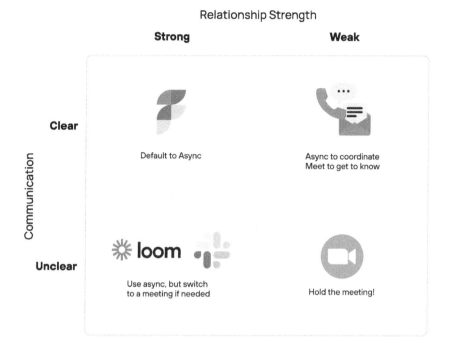

1.) Clear conversation, strong relationship

If you are working with someone you know well and are discussing a straightforward topic, you probably don't need to have a meeting. For example, if I ask a team member to recap the week or share an update on key metrics, they could share this info over email or using a tool like Friday. If something is unclear in the update that is *conveyed*, we may need to *converge* and develop shared meaning in a meeting.

2.) Clear conversation, weak relationship

Now imagine a scenario where you are tasked with presenting a monthly update to a new client. The update is straightforward, but you also don't know the client well. Should you schedule a real-time meeting or send the update in an email instead?

In this example, the relationship is weak, so you may want to schedule a meeting as it's a good chance to get to know each other. It also gives you the chance to provide clarity on material you shared in the written update. Over time, as the relationship strengthens, you may not need to hold the meeting anymore.

3.) Unclear conversation, strong relationship

If you have a good relationship with the recipients, but encounter a vague topic like a strategic conversation or brainstorming session, consider syncing up in Zoom or a real-world meeting.

If you are trying to establish common ground and *converge* around shared meaning, you need a fast feedback loop that a real-time meeting or Slack conversation provides. With that being said, you can accelerate the conversation by sharing information asynchronously *before* you meet.

4.) Unclear conversation, weak relationship

In a situation where you are communicating with someone you don't know well, on a topic that is unclear, you should meet up in person or have a Zoom call. You need to build a better relationship, create clarity, and *converge* around shared meaning.

These are the most complicated conversations you will have and the potential for misunderstanding is high.

For example, imagine you are exploring raising investment from a venture capital firm. You don't know the investor well, and the nature of their involvement seems complicated. Does it make sense to email back and forth, or could the conversation be accelerated by jumping on a Zoom call?

Wrapping up

I hope this chapter provides inspiration for how you can pick the ideal communication method for the job at hand. As the communication theorist Marshall McLuhan once said, *"the medium is the message."*

| 7 |

How to go async-first

One question I hear all the time from leaders is, "how can I shift my company to a remote-first model?" It's easy to talk about, but it's much more difficult to create habits and workflows to operationalize these principles.

In the rest of this chapter, I'm going to share specific workflows to help you shift away from the real-time meetings and never ending Zoom calls towards a more asynchronous or remote-first way of working.

1. Recurring meetings

The first way to go async-first is to improve the effectiveness of recurring meetings, like your weekly team meetings or all-hands meetings.

How it works:

1. Ask your team to share structured, written updates before the meeting
2. Show up to the meeting with updates out of the way, which saves ~20 minutes

3. Use the written updates as a foundation for discussion. Converge around shared meaning and resolve blockers

4. Take notes and share a recap asynchronously with the attendees or other stakeholders who were unable to attend

This topic is so important we've written an entire chapter on it (see - *Chapter 9: How to cut your meetings in half*).

2. Proposals

Now, imagine a project proposal meeting. If you show up to this meeting without enough context, the meeting will be an epic waste of time. Participants will struggle to understand everything in real-time, especially for complex topics.

On the other hand, you could:

- Share the proposal in writing before the meeting, collecting initial thoughts and high-level reactions asynchronously.
- Discuss the written proposal in a meeting, so the entire team is aligned and on the same page
- When the proposal is approved, share out action items and next steps asynchronously in a follow-up email

For example, Amazon is known for requiring that employees write proposals in a 6-page memo format. At the beginning of the meeting, attendees read the memo in silence before discussing it as a group. This workflow helps ensure that everyone has necessary context, which kickstarts better discussion and makes the meeting more effective.

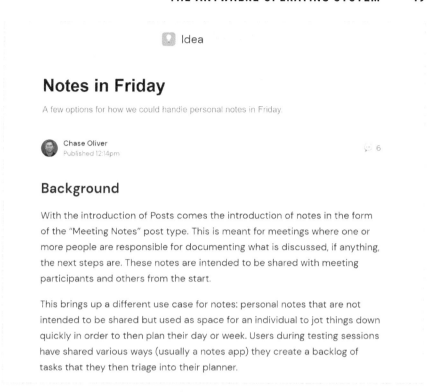

An example of a project proposal in Friday

3. Meeting notes

Another workflow worth trying is to record conversations on Zoom using a tool like Grain.co. You can have a real-time, synchronous conversation with your customers over video and record the conversation so it persists and can be viewed later. You should also take recap notes and summarize the discussion to help communication scale beyond the meeting attendees.

4. Company announcements

Now consider a company-wide announcement. Leaders may share an announcement in a staff meeting, but oftentimes this is quickly forgotten or buried in a random PowerPoint that no one can find.

A simple asynchronous workflow could be to aggregate the company announcements in a written log, so current and future employees can easily review the important announcements that have been made over time. This creates a steady stream of the most important news at the company.

5. Weekly note from the CEO

Another effective asynchronous workflow I've seen from leaders is to share an end of week recap, with sections like:

- What's top of mind
- An update on performance and key metrics
- Other updates

Many leaders will use Slack or email, but I'd recommend against it. There's a lot of noise and competition for attention in these channels, which means that it's unlikely that people will read it. Congratulations, you have officially wasted your time!

I recommend setting up a dedicated space (like an internal blog) that aggregates these posts and provides analytics into how many employees are reading the updates. Additionally, these posts are useful context for new hires, which is why you should keep a running log that can be referenced over time.

Example weekly note in Friday

6. New hire introductions

Speaking of new hires, I've seen many organizations send welcome emails or chat messages when a new hire starts. While this is better than nothing, the announcement is lost and inaccessible for future hires.

Instead, you should have new hires answer questions asynchronously, such as:

- What's one fun fact about you?
- What gives you energy at work?
- What do you enjoy doing outside of work?

Each person at your company should have their own dedicated profile, which displays this information for existing employees and future hires.

In Conclusion

Making the shift to async-first communication is the most important organizational change you and your team can make. The workflows in this chapter are how you do it. It's worth your time to invest in the right tools and processes to make this easy for everyone to do. We'll discuss these ideas in more detail in future chapters.

| 8 |

How to create a company handbook

If you want to be successful from anywhere, you need to create a single source of truth for the most important stuff that everyone should know. Many people call this repository a company handbook. The idea of a handbook has been popularized by all-remote organizations like GitLab (they have a 4,000+ page handbook!)

This information frequently lives in a wiki like Confluence, Notion, Google Docs, or Word. Your company handbook should contain the most important information like:

- History/About
- Mission, Vision, Values
- Annual Goals and KPIs
- Company Policies (Vacation, Holidays, etc.)
- Hiring processes
- Employee/team directory

This handbook aims to provides organizational context, which guides decision making, expected behavior, and helps the entire company level-up. If you don't have a handbook, people will need to gather context over time (through trial and error), which is an epic waste of time and leads to alignment issues.

If you value your time, you should create a handbook, even if it's not perfect. For example, if you are an early stage startup, you may not have clarity on what your company value should be. For many leaders, these are lessons we learn over time. Don't let this stop you. Focus on progress over perfection.

The minimum viable company handbook

If you're looking to get something off the ground quickly, here's a simple framework for you to use:

1. Building Blocks

- Founding story/history of company
- Mission, vision, values
- Who we serve (customer personas)
- Why we are different (unique differentiators)
- Annual goals
- Product principles
- How we hire

2. People and Teams

- Org structure
- People profiles
- Team profiles

3. The day-to-day

- Policies
- How we communicate

- Tools we use
- Standard operating procedures
- Monthly or quarterly goals

I've outlined these sections in a bit more detail below:

Building Blocks

The building blocks outline the most important information. Imagine a new employee who joins your company – what do they *need* to know? In this section, consider including the founding story, the mission, company values, and other foundational principles that guide daily action.

People and Teams

In the people-and-teams section, there should be structure to help everyone navigate the people side of the business. For example, what teams exist inside the company and what is their North Star?

You should also create people profiles for each member of your team where they can add more information, like their personality, hobbies, location, and other information that can help break the ice. When working from anywhere, it can be incredibly difficult to start a conversation with someone you don't know, so you need context to grease the wheels for interesting conversations.

Day-to-day

The day-to-day section aims to encapsulate the information that someone might need to access on an everyday basis. This is for existing employees instead of new hires. Unlike the other sections that rarely change, this content will change much more frequently, which is why it deserves its own section in the handbook.

Potential roadblocks you may run into:

While creating a company handbook is important, there are potential pitfalls for which you will need to be on the lookout:

1. Wikis are like file cabinets

Your team won't regularly visit a wiki unless you constantly point people to it. Knowledge management tools function a bit like a file cabinet. You only access them when you need them.

This lack of visibility can limit effectiveness when you try to reinforce company values and quarterly goals. If these waypoints are not front and center, your team will forget about them, which limits the effectiveness of the handbook.

2. Content can become stale quickly

Another downside of a company wiki is that it's easy to forget to keep them updated. The content becomes stale and out of date.

3. Everyone has an opinion on structure

If you aren't intentional about designing the structure of the wiki, it will get confusing quickly. Everyone has an opinion about content should be structured and it can become chaotic, especially as your company grows. This is why larger organizations will hire dedicated librarians (knowledge management professionals) to help separate the signal from the noise.

As for you, you probably can't afford to hire a full-time librarian. Once again, this is why long-term content should go in one section, and day-to-day content should be located in another. Additionally, you should consider restricting edit access to reduce chaos.

4. A tax on the most productive people

The final point I will make is that wikis tend to be a tax on the most productive people in the organization. If someone is asked the same question over and over, at some point, they will get sick and tired of repeating themselves, so they will write things down in the wiki and share the page instead. You cannot build a successful async-first organization if the only time people want to contribute to a wiki is when they are annoyed with a coworker. There needs to be a better way to get the average person in your company excited about communicating asynchronously. This can't be a ritual that only a small percentage of your company participates in.

Aisha's perspective:

"Starting my first day working at Friday, I was so excited to jump headfirst into the company and start working. My first meeting with Luke was onboarding alongside another intern, where we'd go over the company culture, values, and other important information to know about Friday.

It was really helpful getting the context of the company before starting to work there because I felt I wasn't walking into it blindly. Having never worked remotely before, I was worried about how I'd be able to grasp everything at the company without the extensive paperwork and having the close proximity of my fellow coworkers to ask questions.

Overall it helped me get a sense of what to expect during my time here."

In Conclusion

I'd encourage you to focus most of your energy on how to make your handbook easy to discover and navigate. If you don't do this, you should expect to answer the same questions over and over.

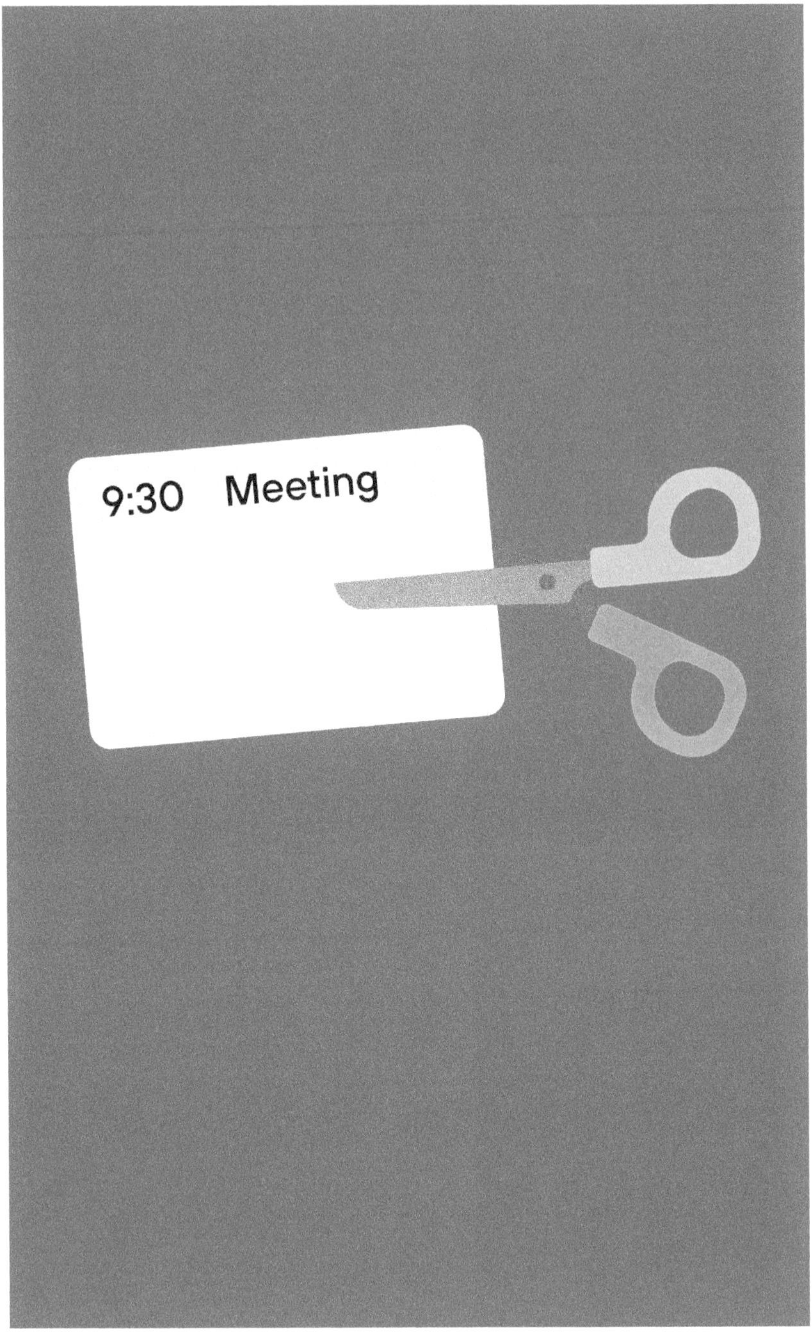
9:30 Meeting

| 9 |

How to cut internal meetings in half

If you consider a flexible workplace where your team can do its best work at a time that makes the most sense for the individual, one of the biggest roadblocks in our way is unnecessary meetings.

External meetings tend to be higher value conversations as you are working with a prospect, customer, or client. These conversations are difficult to ignore and can be a great way to build better relationships.

On the contrary, people regularly complain about how much time they spend in internal meetings with co-workers. The COVID-19 pandemic highlighted this problem. According to Microsoft, the average person spent 10% more time in meetings when shifting to remote at the beginning of the pandemic. Additionally, people spent 18% more time in 1:1 meetings and 10% more time in social team meetings and happy hours.

What if there was an easy way to dramatically reduce the time we spend in internal meetings? What if we could walk into a Monday morning staff meeting and instantly jump into the important conversations, instead of going around in a circle and sharing status updates?

Imagine all the time you'd save!

In the remainder of this chapter, I'm going to show you how to create a predictable process to spend half as much time in internal meetings.

Share asynchronous updates before you meet

The key foundational principle to spending less time in meetings is simple: share written updates before you meet. Meetings are for collaboration, relationship building, and removing blockers, not sharing high-level facts and information.

"I've tried that before, it doesn't work"

I don't want to be the bad guy, but you probably aren't doing it right. At a former employer, we decided to share written updates on a Friday afternoon before our Monday morning staff meeting. It was a great idea! At least in theory.

In reality, it was a disaster.

Each person tasked with sharing a status update had to manually set a calendar reminder to remember to fill out a Microsoft Word document. Some people would adhere, but most of the team would forget. Then, we'd show up to the meeting on Monday and the leader would realize that most of the team didn't write an update. No one had read the updates either.

So, what did we do? The team lead resorted to doing what any rational person would do...they went around in a circle asking everyone to share what they were working on.

At this point, the small group of people who prepared and followed directions would become demoralized. They wasted their time compiling a written update! This negative feedback loop compounds and, over time, everyone stops sharing written updates, leaving you demoralized.

Too many points of failure!

The reason why sharing updates before you meet rarely works is because the process requires too much manual effort. There are many ways this seemingly simple process can break down.

For example:

- Participants need to set a reminder to share the update, which may or may not happen.

- A busy team leader doesn't have time to chase after people and remind them to share an update. This is a waste of time.

- The update is most relevant and important for the leader, while individual contributors may feel like they don't need to know everything that's going on with everyone on the team.

- It takes time to remember and share what you accomplished. People will spend time digging through their email, calendar, and task apps to remember what they accomplished over the past week.

- The leader may need to manually collate the updates into a digestible and shareable report, especially if their boss (or another external stakeholder) wants to know what the team is working on. This is time consuming and not fun.

- If you want your team to show up prepared, you will need to share out the report before the meeting and hope everyone reads it.

Can you see why this great idea rarely works in real life? There's too many ways this good idea could go wrong.

A better option

I'd encourage you not to ditch the idea of sharing updates before you meet; but, instead, offload as much of the boring stuff to a computer to help you automate and reduce the potential points of failure.

For example:

- What if there was an easy way to ping your entire team to share an update? Ideally, this ping could be sent in a tool like Slack or Microsoft Teams so it would rise above the noise of a busy email inbox.

- When people share updates, what if the work was automatically pulled into view without needing to visit other apps and project management tools?

- What if the updates were highly structured and filled with context, so you could tease out information vs. collecting vague agenda items and placeholders for future discussion?

- What if you could automatically ping people who have not responded without annoying the people who already shared an update?

- What if there was a way to make sharing updates more fun and rewarding for your team vs. being perceived as a chore?

- What if the updates were automatically compiled into a shareable report AND pushed out to your team before the meeting happens?

If you reduce the barriers to sharing information on a regular basis, you can create a more predictable flow to your communication.

To use an analogy, think of plumbing in a home. The pipes feed water throughout the home, but you also need pumps to instill logic for when water should move from one location to another.

If you don't have pumps, you will get a flood of water in one location and a trickle in another. This is what happens at work – you may be overwhelmed by the constant pings from your immediate team in chat (a flood of information), but you may feel like you have no idea what's going on in another part of the company (a trickle).

Likewise, you need to create systems and repeatability in the way that you communicate. Email, workplace chat, and Zoom are like pipes that enable the flow of communication, but you need pumps to create predictability.

Routines for Success

While there is no perfect solution, we use the software we build at Friday to automate asynchronous updates. We only have three regularly scheduled meetings a month with this playbook:

1. Weekly Kickoff

On Monday at 11 a.m. (in each person's respective timezone), we ask the entire company the following questions asynchronously:

- How was your weekend?
- What do you aim to accomplish this week?

The answers to these questions are a mixture of work and fun, exactly what you might discuss in a weekly staff meeting. People will regularly share photos of a hike or family event; but, as a leader, I also can see what people aim to accomplish. This creates accountability, but also helps me privately course-correct and nudge if there's something more important that someone needs to tackle.

You can use this routine to supplement or eliminate your Monday morning staff meeting.

2. Daily Standup

Throughout the week, we also have a daily standup where we ask the following questions at 9 a.m.:

- What did you accomplish yesterday?
- What are you working on today?
- Anything else you'd like to share?

In all honesty, this is probably the least useful routine we run because it's so tactical and in the weeds, but it's also a great way for people to share their work. The last question gives everyone the opportunity to share if they will be out for an appointment or break.

You can use this routine to supplement or replace your daily standups/huddles.

3. Friday Check-In

Unlike other routines that are transparent and visible to the group, I run another routine that is only visible to me, called the *Friday Check-In*. At the end of the week, the people who report to me can quickly answer the following questions:

- How did you feel about the week? (emoji question)
- How productive do you think you were this week? (1-10 scale)

- What went well this week?
- What was the worst part of your week? Anything I can do to help?

These questions may sound similar to questions you might ask in a 1-1 meeting, which is what this routine aims to complement or replace.

What's cool about this routine is that if you give people some time to collect their thoughts, they will give you amazing feedback and insight that you would not normally get in a face-to-face interaction.

You can then use the information that your team shares asynchronously to kickstart better conversations instead of awkwardly spending the first fifteen minutes trying to figure out what's going on.

If you use this routine, you can hold on-demand 1:1 meetings and have targeted discussions instead of holding meetings where you show up, only to realize that everything is great and you didn't need to have the meeting at all.

Greg Jamrog for **Friday Check-In**   Mar 26th

How did you feel about the week?

🫤

How productive were you this week?

6 out of 10

What went well this week?

Lots of team signups. Now to get more of them to engage

More fine tuning of helpdocs

What was the worst part of your week? Anything I can do to help?

Was hoping for more contact from customers. Staying patient

Add a comment

An example check-in response that deserves a meeting.

4. Monthly Review

At the end of the month, we'll review the past month and look forward to what we need to accomplish next. We ask the following questions asynchronously:

- How effective do you think we were this month? (1-10 scale)
- What is the reason for your score? (1-10 scale)
- What do you think WE should work on next month?
- What do you think YOU should work on next month?

The responses to this monthly routine help me cut down prep time for monthly kickoff meetings. It also helps me understand what each person would like to focus on in the month ahead.

"Asking people to share async updates is impersonal!"

There is no perfect solution and I'm not going to pretend that this approach is perfect for every company.

With that being said, I would argue that the benefits of async updates are much greater than the downside. Your employees are tired of spending their day on video calls and bad meetings (Zoom fatigue anyone?). If you can create an environment where your team has more time to do meaningful work or have the flexibility to take a break because they don't have a useless status update meeting, that's a great outcome for all!

This matters when you work with people across time zones. There is never a good time to hold a meeting for everyone. Someone may take a call early in the day, while another person may need to jump on a call late in the evening.

A few more tips:

If you decide to automate asynchronous updates, make sure to:

- **Acknowledge the response** — if someone shares a great update, make sure you thank them for it. If you use a tool like Friday, you can leave an emoji or comment so they know the message has been received.
- **Remember that meetings are a tool in your toolbox** — the goal here isn't to eliminate all your meetings. It's to have fewer, better meetings.

Aisha's perspective

"Friday was the first company at which I worked where I could respond to automated routines. Before, at my office jobs, I had my boss constantly check up on me to make sure I was staying on track. It certainly helped me stay focused, but I kind of got too comfortable.

When the pandemic hit, it became harder and harder to get the work done, not only because of COVID-19, but also because I no longer had that constant presence behind me.

During my time at Friday, I respond to different routines. The Daily Standup is one I use a lot, and it helps keep me on track. I write out everything I have to do, and I even write what I accomplished the day before. It's a good reminder of what I have to do, and also the progress I made along the way. Not only is my progress viewable to me, but I can also view my coworkers' Daily Standup as well. It's cool to see what everyone else is doing. I focus more on the marketing side of Friday, so it's nice to see the design side, or the product side that my coworkers handle.

One thing I greatly enjoy about Friday's routines is the ability to answer icebreakers at the end of completing a routine. Just like how you would talk to and get to know a coworker during your in-person lunch break, icebreakers let me know more about my coworkers that are unrelated to work. It definitely helps me feel like I'm connected to the team, and

I'm more willing to share things in the hopes that someone else will relate!"

In Conclusion

If you disconnect information sharing from meetings, you will spend less time in meetings. This isn't rocket science. Meetings are best for building relationships, removing blockers, and brainstorming. Stick to that. Your team will thank you.

| 10 |

How to build company culture

The number of ping-pong tables at the office does not create a healthy company culture. In a remote-first world, a Slack channel where employees can talk about their pets is not your company culture either.

If we want to truly understand how to build a strong company culture when remote, we need to first understand what culture even means.

What is culture?

One of my favorite definitions of culture is by Edgar Schein in the book, *Organizational Culture and Leadership*:

> "Organizational culture is the pattern of basic assumptions that a given group has invented, discovered, or developed in learning to cope with its problems of external adaptation and internal integration, and that have worked well enough to be considered valid, and, therefore, to be taught to new members as the correct way to perceive, think, and feel in relation to those problems."

He breaks down culture further, which I've summarized below:

1. Artifacts

Artifacts are visible, observable signs. They could be specific rituals, habits, the language you use, and behavior that your team exhibits on a regular basis. These artifacts can be observed by outsiders.

2. Values

Values are shared opinions about the way things should be. The most obvious example of shared opinions are company values that aim to guide behavior and how you hire (and who you need to let go). If artifacts are the "what," then values are "why" you act and behave in a particular way.

3. Basic Assumptions

Basic assumptions are another level deeper than values. These are principles that everyone takes for granted and is never challenged by the group. For example, the importance of spending time with each other, how people should relate to each other, and more.

Defining your company culture

The reason why it is so important to define your culture is because if you don't, you will look at artifacts (like a ping pong table at the office or a Slack channel) and will incorrectly label this as your culture.

You've only peeled back one layer of the onion!

If you want to dig deeper and better define your company culture, consider getting your team together and completing a group exercise where you:

1. **Document the artifacts** — write down the unique behaviors, norms, and other observable things your company does

2. **Ask "WHY do we do this?"** — this will help you unpack the company values and shared beliefs.

3. **Match artifacts with values and identify gaps** — Sometimes you will see that you behave in a way that doesn't line up with your values. It's important to dig deeper into these gaps that exist, as it may mean you need to iterate on your values.

How it works

At Friday, here's a few behaviors that you may observe if you join the company as a new hire:

- We dislike regularly scheduled internal meetings (3 per month, with 2/3 being unrelated to work)
- In every async update we share, there's an opportunity to share something personal
- We try to build products that feel fun
- We try not to take ourselves too seriously

Why do we act this way?

One of our company values is that we aim to be **autonomous by default**. Our goal with this value is to enable everyone in the company to run at their own pace.

If you look at the everyday behaviors (the artifacts), there's a little bit of a disconnect here.

This disconnect happens because the basic assumption lurking beneath the surface is that **we believe every day at work should feel a bit**

more like Friday. We spend 40+ hours a week working, why can't we make this time feel more like the last day of the work week?

The reason why we try to be autonomous by default (a company value) is because we want to give people time and space to do their best work. Another basic assumption we have at Friday is that *doing your best work drives happiness, not the other way around.*

This simple exercise can help you quickly understand what's really driving group behavior at your company. While you will never be able to perfectly articulate your company values, the key ingredient is to constantly discuss and iterate on them.

Reinforcing cultural values

At this point, you should have a clear understanding of how to define and convey your company values in a nuanced way without saying "we have ping-pong tables and fun Slack channels." The next step is the more difficult part. How do you constantly reinforce these values when everyone isn't in the same room?

If we think about the culture framework, previously we were trying to peel back the layers and identify the basic assumptions. Now, we are trying to reinforce the values into everyday behavior. We want to work in the opposite direction.

Why does this matter?

Your company values glue the organization together. They shape behavior, how you hire, and who you may need to fire. If you don't have glue, things will fall apart.

Values must be constantly reinforced

The first step to reinforcing your culture values is to make your values visible and easily referenced. This is much tougher to implement than it sounds.

Here are a few examples of how to reinforce your values at work:

- Before you hire someone, you should ask questions based on your company values and determine if there's alignment. You could also highlight these values on your company website and job pages.

- When you onboard someone new, you should reiterate these values right away

- Values should be front and center in your company handbook

- If you have an office, values could be displayed on the wall or a bulletin board

- When you do monthly reviews or quarterly planning, you should reiterate the company values

What may surprise you is that most of your company will not remember this stuff. According to research, 95% of a company's employees are unaware of, or do not understand, its strategy. While this statistic is unfortunate, it's entirely predictable. Values tend to be aspirational and can be too abstract to shape everyday behavior.

Your values must be integrated into the everyday

After reinforcing values, the next step is to incorporate them into everyday behaviors. It's not enough to talk about what's important. You will need to live them out.

For example:

- When hiring, create structured interview questions based on company values for potential recruits.

- If you use tools to share recognition/kudos, make sure you can tag a company value. Even better, there should be analytics to show if you are trending in the right direction or not.

- Performance reviews or annual reviews should incorporate questions to verify that people are living out the company values.

- If you need to make a difficult decision, list out the appropriate values at the top of a decision document or at the beginning of the meeting.

 Chase Oliver gave 👏 **Kudos** to **Tanvi Modi**   May 25th

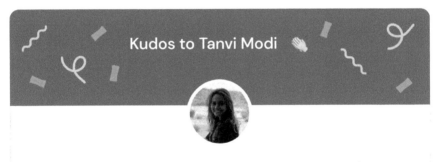

Really fun to see the planner visualizations progressing. Can't wait to see them with my own data!

#autonomous   #originalthinking

🙏 1   • 2 comments

Example kudos with a tagged value

Please keep in mind that it's okay if your company values are aspirational. Values are a forcing function for who you want to be and how you aim to behave. It's not about being perfect, it's about striving to be better than yesterday.

Aisha's perspective

"Giving kudos at Friday is a brand new experience for me. At my past in-person internship, my boss and coworkers thanked me for completing my work as I finished it. Now working remotely, I wasn't sure how that was going to translate over.

Friday gives you a chance to send kudos publicly or privately to different people on your team, while also tagging one or more of the company values. On my first day of work, I received some kudos from my coworkers, welcoming me to the team. It made me feel like I was already part of the team. I've received kudos for doing great work, and I sent kudos to others for the same reason—whether I was impressed with what I'd seen, someone helped me out personally, or just because I felt like it that day.

I really think it's nice to receive kudos, because it feels like all the progress you've put into work has been seen by others. It's satisfying that even though we don't see each other face-to-face, we can still feel connected."

| 11 |

How to feel connected to your team

Another issue you will need to confront is feeling disconnected from your team. Before, you could walk into the office and feel the energy as you walked around. Now, you may try to engage the team through Zoom and it feels different. Sometimes you may try to be engaging on a Zoom call, but you get blank stares and silence from the group. Does anyone even care?

I get it. The fact that everyone isn't together in one room makes running a business feel a lot more abstract. I can't "influence" and energize my team like I might be able to in person. Is the energetic feeling a nice-to-have or a must-have though? I understand if you want to create an engaging place to work. I do, too. I have worked for companies where the office felt like a party atmosphere and while it was fun at times, we also had high turnover and the company ended up failing. The positive vibes didn't matter in the end.

In this chapter, we're going to teach you some tactics to feel more connected to your team. The goal is to make sure that your coworkers feel more like people and less like words on a screen.

Asynchronous

The tips in this section help you learn more about your coworkers, without requiring a meeting. If creating a feeling of connection can only be accomplished with another meeting, you are creating a potential bottleneck.

Create people profiles

You should start by having every employee create a people profile. Think of this profile as a mashup of your LinkedIn and Facebook profile. The goal is to create context about who you are and how you like to work, which is especially important when you onboard new hires. These profiles build a bedrock of empathy and remind you that your coworkers are real people, not emotionless robots.

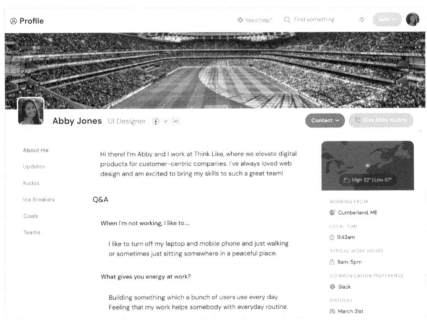

An example "people profile" in Friday

I'd strongly recommend the following sections in your profile:

1. Personal user manual

Personal user manuals have become a bit of a fad over the past couple of years, but the basic idea is that you can proactively answer questions to help coworkers understand your quirks, how you work, and what makes you unique. It's like a user manual for how to work with you.

For example, you might answer questions like:

- What gives you energy at work?

- What drains you at work?

- How do you like to receive feedback?

- How can someone earn a gold star with you?

- What might someone misunderstand about you?

While these user manuals can become too prescriptive when left unchecked, they can also dramatically accelerate relationship-building for the group.

2. Personality

Whether you love personality tests or think they are hocus pocus, I'd recommend taking one. The purpose of a personality test is NOT to be prescriptive. They exist to provide a mental framework for understanding that people are different and that differences are a healthy thing. This exercise leads to deep, engaging conversations that help you get to know your team.

Additionally, when you combine a personality test with a user manual, you get a nice mixture of open-ended responses from the manual, while the personality test provides more structure. These two frameworks complement each other.

There are a variety of personality frameworks you could try, like:

- Enneagram

- DISC

- Myers Briggs

- True Colors

I recommend DISC. The Enneagram is a useful conversation starter and goes deeper than DISC, but it's a bit more unfiltered, which may not be ideal for work. I recommend using CrystalKnows.com to generate personality results, generate group reports, and more.

2. Icebreakers

Another way to feel connected is by sprinkling icebreakers into existing rituals. At Friday, we use our software to periodically answer icebreakers after completing a daily standup or weekly update. This provides a steady stream of useful tidbits about your coworkers. It's like a digital version of having an interesting discussion at the water-cooler in the office.

What was your first job?

First thing I got paid for was working at my school over the summer making $8/hour to move a bunch of stuff around to prep for next school year. Favorite memories include:

- Janitor Kevin telling us that he beat a Corvette off the line with his Geo Metro - we assumed the Corvette did not know they were racing
- Janitor Kevin telling us his grandpa (or uncle) used to say "Work smarter, not harder."

First real job was Nashville shores. Worked in the grounds department which involved walking the entire park all day picking up trash, dumping trash cans, and other fun activities. All while everyone else is having fun swimming and I was wearing khakis and a red polo shirt (mad farmers tan). Favorite memories include:

Hrmmm okay

3. Say thanks on a regular basis

Everyone knows that they should say thanks a bit more often, but it's easy to forget this simple, yet important activity. Is it possible to turn this into a habit?

Yup.

If you use Friday to share daily standups or a weekly update, you will get a prompt at the end, encouraging you to send kudos. This dramatically improves the likelihood that you will send recognition as it's baked into an existing habit.

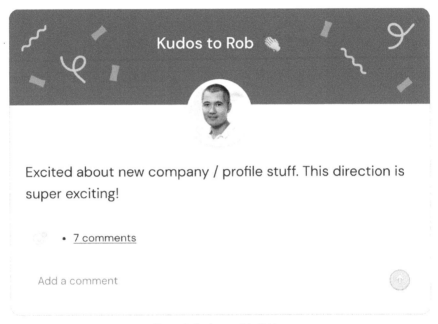

Example kudos sent in Friday

People love it when coworkers make an intentional effort to thank them. I'm sure you will find the same with your team.

Synchronous

Next, we have ways to feel connected that revolve around meetings. These events should be intentional and well-planned. If you schedule a team-building event at 10 p.m. for a coworker, they probably won't enjoy it.

Flip some of your meetings upside down

Typically, meetings at work start with a few minutes of small talk, followed by discussion of work. I'd encourage you to create a few meetings where the format *is the exact opposite.*

Instead of small talk at the beginning, you could start with work and then spend the rest of the time doing team building. Instead of spending 5% of meeting time hanging out, you should hang out 95% of the time instead.

To illustrate how this format works, we hold a one-hour meeting every two weeks that we call, "coffee shop co-working." The basic idea is that we try to create a time to hang out like we might if we were all huddled around a table at a coffee shop.

The purpose of this meeting is to hang out, play games, and talk about work a little bit. While there is no replacement for hanging out in person, I really enjoy this time and it's an awesome way to learn more about my coworkers.

The format of this hangout varies, but it resembles something like this:

- **10-15 minutes** — show and tell. You can share something cool you are working on for the benefit of the broader group
- **10-15 minutes** — brainstorming around a particular problem or area of opportunity that is relevant to the entire group
- **30 minutes** — play games

I always end these meetings feeling like I could go another hour. They are a ton of fun.

Play games

Playing games may sound cheesy, but it's much better than awkward team building sessions where you go around in a circle and answer lame questions about yourself in front of everyone else. You need to create an environment where people can let their guard down and have a bit of fun. Games is how you make this happen.

I recommend the following options:

1. Skribbl

Skribbl is online Pictionary. One person draws a picture and everyone needs to guess the correct word within a limited amount of time. While this sounds cheesy at first blush, it's a lot of fun.

2. Gartic Phone

Gartic Phone is like the telephone game meets Pictionary. Someone on your team writes a statement, and someone else needs to draw it. This process repeats itself and involves a lot of laughs. Without a doubt, this is the funniest game I've ever played with the Friday team. The makers (Onrizon social games) have other fun games worth trying, so make sure to check those out too.

3. Quiplash

Next up, we have Quiplash. Quiplash allows two or more people to answer prompts and the audience picks a winner. You can discover who is sarcastic, witty, and more.

4. Airbnb Online Experiences

Another option is an Airbnb online experience. Basically, it's a group Zoom call where you can learn about something interesting, like how to make an epic cup of coffee, what it's like to live in New Zealand on a goat farm, and more.

5. Cribs: work-from-home edition

Finally, you might consider having teammates share house or home office tours, like you are the host of MTV Cribs.

The point of these team-building events is to kickstart conversation and make it easy to get to know your team. If this feels forced, continue to iterate until you find something the team enjoys.

5. Friday afternoon happy hour

Another option is to hold a happy hour on a Friday afternoon. I've heard of some companies playing video games during this time. Several of our customers do this and seem to enjoy it. Once again, make sure you are being thoughtful about when these events occur, especially if your team is scattered across several time zones.

Aisha's perspective

"Along with reading my coworkers' icebreaker answers every morning, one thing I really appreciate about Friday are the co-working coffee workshops we do bi-weekly. We all come together over Zoom for an hour to take a break from work and just simply connect.

This is the first company I worked at where I had meetings to connect with people instead of sharing progress updates. We spend the first 30 minutes catching up with one another, and we have the chance to share updates on things we're working on. The last 30 minutes are spent on online multiplayer games.

We played Skribbl for the first few weeks. It was so hilarious to try to guess what everyone was attempting to draw. Sometimes we typed out random guesses because there was no way of knowing what was on our screens.

The next game we played is called Quiplash. I never played this game before, so I was lost at the beginning; but once I got the idea, I loved it. Coming up with random phrases and voting on them is such a breath of fresh air during long work days.

My absolute favorite game we played is called Gartic Phone. It's a telephone game where everyone writes out a prompt, and the next person has to draw it out. The next person has to write a prompt for the drawing. It gets passed down, like a telephone, and we see how well we were able to keep the original prompt. Some of the prompts were absolutely hilarious, and the drawings that followed were similar. I haven't laughed as much as I did in a while, and it was such an enjoyable time for all of us. It was a co-working call well spent!"

What about meeting up in person?

Don't worry, we have a dedicated chapter for company meetups later in this book!

MONDAY

Weekly Goal

Daily Standup #1

Daily Standup #2

Daily Standup #3

Friday Check-in

FRIDAY

| 12 |

How to create accountability from afar

As your organization learns to work-from-anywhere, you may wonder how you can create a sense of accountability.

You want to believe that your team will work on the most important things and that you can be hands-off. At the same time, you need to create an environment where everyone feels a sense of responsibility for their output. To use a sports analogy: as a coach, you have a responsibility to call the play, but you also need to let the team run the play, too.

Why is it tough to create accountability when remote?

There's a few reasons why you may struggle to create accountability when apart. Here's a few factors to consider:

1. Fewer data points and observational cues

As I discussed earlier in the book, when you are in the office, it's easy to learn through osmosis and manage by walking around. Now, you have less data to observe. As a result, you feel out of the loop.

2. Fewer opportunities to nudge

In the best book I've ever read on leading a team (*High Output Management*), Andy Grove shares that nudging is one of the most important activities a leader can do. Here's how he describes it:

> "You often do things at the office designed to influence events slightly, maybe making a phone call to an associate suggesting that a decision be made in a certain way...In such instances you may be advocating a preferred course of action, but you are not issuing an instruction or a command."

It's easy to nudge people when you are all in the same place. Additionally, these quick chats can help people stay aligned and accountable.

3. Commitments are too vague and easily forgotten

This issue happens at the office, too, but it's easy to tell a colleague in a meeting that you will do something, only to forget about it. A while later, each person has a different recollection of what was discussed and there's nothing to reference, which creates frustration.

This breakdown can lead to a feeling that people aren't taking responsibility for their actions.

The building blocks for accountability

Let's build a conceptual model for how we can fix the problems mentioned above. At a high level, accountability is defined as a willingness to accept responsibility or to account for one's actions.

If you say you will do something, will you actually do it? Let's break this down into a few components:

1. A commitment to perform an activity in the future

This first part is not rocket science. You need to share what you aim to accomplish in a specific timeframe.

Example commitments:

- "I will ship this code by the end of today"
- "I send the status report before your next meeting"

The format is straightforward and should be written: **I will do [activity] by [due date]**. Research shows that if you write down your goals, you are 42% more likely to achieve them.

2. Sharing progress along the way

This next part isn't required, but is certainly helpful as it can be difficult for others to know what the current status of a project. If someone on your team isn't proactively sharing this information, it's likely that you will wonder, "how is that project going?" Eventually, you will ask about it.

If you are like me, you hate asking people for an update, but you also need to have insight so you can course correct and nudge if projects get off track.

3. Delivery, reflection, and inspection

One of the most important components of accountability is delivering on what you said you would do. If you said you would have something done by the end of the day, did you get it done? If not, why?

Missing deadlines is a reality of work that will never go away, which is why reflection and continuously improving should be the aim. How will you improve tomorrow?

4. A little peer pressure along the way

Similar to writing your goals, research shows that when you share a goal with others, you are more likely to accomplish it. This is because you feel a sense of peer pressure. You told a coworker you would do something and you don't want to let them down.

Can we systematize accountability?

Using these components, can we create repeatable systems for staying accountable? I've tried to use project management tools to accomplish this goal, but it rarely becomes a habit without herculean amounts of effort. Is there a better way?

I think so. Here's what we do.

1. Establish weekly priorities on Monday

At the beginning of the week, each person on our team answers two questions in Friday:

- How was your weekend? (open-ended)
- What do you aim to accomplish by the end of the week? (open-ended)

The answers are shared with the entire company. The first question is fun, but the second question sets a foundation for the result that we can expect from each teammate by the end of the week. As a leader, I am able to understand where each person is pointed, and, if I need to nudge them in another direction, I can do this early in the week.

Josh Spilker for 📖 **Weekly Goal**   Apr 12th

How was your weekend?

My parents took the kids overnight to a campground on
Saturday, so that was a nice break.

And I did a short hike and a lot of reading

What do you plan on accomplishing this week?

* publish 3 to 5 pieces
* assign 3–4 creative briefs
* clean up a couple of video transcriptions to publish
* answer Quora q's
* double check a few Ahrefs site audit tasks

Add a comment

An example weekly goal response

2. Share progress with daily standups

Next, every day at 9 a.m., each person quickly shares an update for the
following questions:

- What did you accomplish yesterday? (open-ended)
- What are you working on today? (open-ended)
- Anything else you'd like to share? (open-ended)

These answers are shared publicly too. This helps everyone see what's going on *right now*. It also helps create a habit of being thoughtful about how you allocate your time.

3. Recap your week

At the end of the week, on Friday, we ask a few more questions:

- How did you feel about the week (emoji)

- How productive were you this week? (1-10 scale)

- What went well? (open-ended)

- What was the worst part of your week? Is there anything I can do to help? (open-ended)

Unlike other routines, this is only viewed by me. Because these answers aren't shared with the broader group, there's less filtering that happens, which gives incredible insight into what's really going on at work and helps kickstart more effective 1:1 conversations and fix potential problems.

Why does this work?

If you think about it, people have used habit journals and planners to accomplish similar outcomes for personal productivity. We are using the same principles in a team setting. If we use the accountability framework listed earlier in the chapter, we are:

- **Making commitments** at the beginning of the week (Monday priorities)

- **Sharing progress** along the way (via daily standups)

- **Reflecting** at the end of the week and making adjustments (Friday recap)

Most importantly, these routines involve writing commitments down and sharing them with others, which we know improves the likelihood that people will hit their goals.

To wrap up, we've created a repeatable system for staying accountable. If you adopt a similar set of routines, I'm sure you will find success as well!

Aisha's Perspective

"Doing daily routines with Friday really helps me stay accountable with myself. It's easy to fall into the trap of walking into your day blindly, especially when working remotely. There's no longer someone behind your back making sure you get the work done.

When doing the routines, I'm forcing myself to address my tasks. I tell myself what I want to accomplish during the week. During my daily standups, I showcase my day-to-day progress. At the end of the week, I see how that week went.

Unlike my other in-person jobs, I am the one in control of my progress and accomplishments. It's a great feeling of being able to come up with my own priorities at work, and seeing them through to completion. And while it does benefit me personally, I feel like it also helps the team. Sharing tasks with everyone else makes me more willing to want to do it. Also, if I'm ever stuck on something, the team is willing to help me because I share my progress."

Name: ???

Ability: 34
Reliability: 40
Rapport: 20

Status: Weirded out by the staring

Have a 1-1 conversation

Give them training

Hang out with them

Trust meter

Ask for their name (again)

Low

High

| 13 |

How to build trusted work relationships

Now, let's talk about another pain point that you may feel but may not want to admit - trusting your team. You may read advice on how you need to build trust with your team when working remotely.

What does this even mean?

Does this mean you should do virtual trust-fall sessions? Statements like, "you should build trust" is too vague to be useful. I'm going to do my best to provide some clarity here.

What is trust?

Trust is defined as: *firm belief in the reliability, truth, ability, or strength of someone or something.*

Accountability (discussed in the previous chapter) is about having faith that the work will get done. Trust is a belief *in the person* who's doing the work. If we want to build trust from apart, how do we do it?

The building blocks of trust

I think about trust in the same way I think about a math equation. My theory is that there are three main factors that you can control, and one factor over which you don't have a lot of control:

$$\textbf{TRUST} = (\ \text{Ability} + \text{Reliability} + \text{Rapport}\ ) \times \text{Time}$$

Trust is like a math equation!

1. Ability

Is the person skilled at what they do? Are they capable of doing the work? Do they have the expertise required?

If someone doesn't have the skillset for what's required in the role, trust will erode because you won't believe that they are capable of performing the work required.

2. Reliability

Can you trust that the person will deliver on what they said they would do? If someone does what they say, your level of trust in the person will grow, as they will establish a track record of being reliable.

3. Rapport

Also known as empathy, I think about rapport as having the ability to mentally walk in someone else's shoes. Can you empathize with why someone made a particular decision? Do you understand what motivated them to make a decision?

My favorite example to illustrate this point is a quote from Abraham Lincoln:

"I don't like that man. I must get to know him better."

This quote highlights that it's easy to dislike someone or not trust them if you don't know them. If you don't have rapport with your team, it's easy to assume the worst because you are too disconnected from reality.

4. Time

The fourth variable is time, which is something over which you don't have much control. I included this as the multiplier in the equation because it impacts all the other variables in the trust equation. Spending more time with your team members can help you build rapport and become more empathetic. It can help you understand what talents someone has. It can also help you understand how reliable they are.

So how do you build trust?

If we want to build trust, we need to move the needle on the trust equation. I've outlined ways you can do this below:

1. Improve ability

If you want to improve skill and ability, you need to invest in training, mentorship, or you need to find a job for the person that better matches their strengths.

2. Improve reliability

If you want to improve reliability, consider creating systems that improve accountability as described in the previous chapter. You may want to consider investing in tooling like Friday to systematize accountability.

3. Improve rapport

If you want to improve rapport, you should:

- **Have regular 1:1 conversations** — this will help you understand what makes people tick and how they are feeling about their work.

- **Complete a people profile** — see a user manual for how someone works, see their personality and other facts to remind you that you work with people, not robots.

- **Hang out** — see the chapter on feeling connected to your team for more specific recommendations.

4. Time?

In the trust equation, I shared that time is the multiplier for building trust. Oddly enough, time can boost or chip away at trust. For example, if someone is unreliable, over time you will collect more data and become more convinced of your intuition.

I'd encourage you not to think of time in terms of weeks or months, but instead, the depth of relationship you are able to build with someone.

Aisha's perspective

"Building trust with the team was something I strove for when starting work at Friday. At my previous job, even though I was working remotely, we started off working in person. I knew of all my coworkers and their work habits, so it wasn't jarring when I switched to remote work.

At Friday, we do bi-weekly coffee shop coworking meetings where we learn more about each other. I've also met up with Luke in person a couple of times instead of having a virtual meeting. I enjoyed just grabbing a coffee and walking along the beach while we talked about work and also random stuff. That helped build the idea that I can trust my team, because we can engage in these activities. Working remotely does not equal separating yourself from everyone else, as I once feared. There are ways to stay connected in more ways than just all being in an office."

In conclusion

You need to trust your team if you want to do amazing work. I hope you use the framework in this chapter as inspiration on how you can improve ability, reliability, and rapport. Just remember, this won't happen overnight.

| 14 |

Staying aligned

Similar to accountability and trust, alignment is a vague word that means different things to different people. When I think about alignment, I think about a sports team. The coach is responsible for coordinating the entire group and achieving a high level of performance, but each player has a specific position to play. Players are divided into smaller groups (i.e., offense vs. defense), but the entire team has a mission – to win the game.

The best companies operate like a high-performing team, but what does this look like when working from anywhere? In the rest of this chapter, we're going to talk about **roles** and **goals**, the building blocks for staying aligned.

Roles

Every person needs to understand what position they need to play on the field. Some people are responsible for scoring. Others are responsible for preventing goals from being scored.

When hiring, most organizations will create a job posting and highlight a list of responsibilities to help candidates understand what is required of them. While this is helpful during the hiring process, the job description becomes stale and outdated quickly. To make matters worse, this information is not shared with existing employees, so they have no idea why someone is working at the company.

"Who is responsible for _____?

Who should I talk to to learn about _____"

"What would you say you do here?"

A good question!

The lack of transparency in roles and responsibilities can cause unintended consequences. A new hire is trying to make an impact, but they don't know if they overstepped their bounds. I can't tell you how many times I've unintentionally made this mistake in the past.

How to fix it?

I've found the following activities can make a huge difference:

- **Give people clear areas of ownership and don't overcomplicate it.** Often you hire people to solve one primary pain point. Make it obvious what the most important area of ownership is.

- **Make key responsibilities visible to all** – Ideally, a new employee should be able to visit a coworker's profile and see what they are responsible for. They shouldn't need to ask around to learn this.

Goals

Now, let's talk about goals. In almost 10 years of working remotely (for a variety of companies, both big and small), I've never seen a single company do this well. It's not a lack of effort. It's because it's tricky to align an entire group of people towards a common objective.

How goal-setting works now

As a leadership team, you will meet up toward the end of the year, spend a day or two in meetings, lightning will strike, and the perfect goals will float down from the sky. Then, you will encourage team leaders to do the same with their staff, making sure that team goals "ladder-up" to the company objectives.

At the end of this exercise, you are feeling pretty great. You can see all the goals and success metrics in a spreadsheet. You are a genius.

Two weeks later, reality hits. Things change. You need to revisit your assumptions and adapt the plan. The beautiful spreadsheet becomes stale. In a meeting, you ask a team leader to share progress on an OKR and they stare at you with a look of terror.

Problems

After watching this bad movie over and over, I'd argue that there's three major issues with this approach:

- **Out of sight, out of mind** – when important goals are buried in a document, it's easy to forget about them. Out of sight, out of mind.

- **Not transparent & accessible to all** – The goal doc is crafted for your benefit, not the average employee. This information is rarely packaged in a way that resonates with the front line. As a result, they don't care about it.

- **Doesn't reflect the current state** – You oftentimes need to beg your team to update the current status. It's easy to forget, which means the information becomes stale. This is a recipe for the dreaded status update meeting.

What to do?

While there is no silver bullet that will work for every company, here are a few principles to follow:

1. Goals cannot live in a spreadsheet

To start, you need to get goals and initiatives out of hidden spreadsheets that no looks at. To use an analogy from the office environment, should this information be stashed away in a file cabinet or displayed on a bulletin board?

If you store goals in a spreadsheet, you are asking your team to forget about them. This information needs to be in an easy-to-access place and visible *at least once a week*. You should constantly refer to your goals in meetings, but you need to make sure you've stored it in a way that can easily be accessed by anyone, at any time.

2. Goals need to be centralized in one place

A growing number of project management tools (Asana, Jira, etc.) offer goals functionality in their products. Resist the urge to use one of these tools to document and report on goals. As your company grows, each team will want to use its own project management tool. This fragmentation creates a lack of visibility and makes it impossible to centralize goals in one place for all to see. As a result, you will need to hold meetings to understand what's going on.

3. Each goal needs to have a directly responsible individual

Next up, every goal needs to have an owner who is responsible for sharing progress. This is known as the directly responsible individual (DRI). Without an owner, there is no accountability.

4. Goals must be integrated into everyday workflows

It's not enough to stash your goals in one place. You need to be able to look and see exactly what is going on at a given moment in time. Every DRI must share progress on a regular basis. The most obvious way to collect this information is to hold a meeting, but, as you may recall from previous chapters, sharing information and status updates is best done asynchronously.

What we do at Friday

At Friday, we use our goals product to centralize and report on key initiatives.

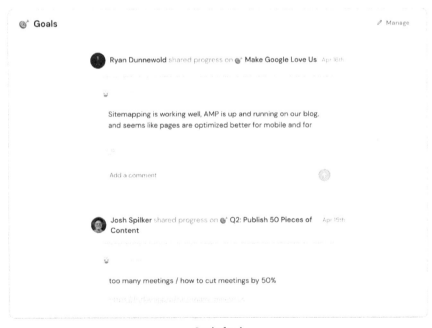

Goals in one place

We already use the product for daily standups, weekly updates, and more, so directly responsible individuals can easily report on goal progress once a week after sharing an update.

As people share progress, this information is pushed into a goals newsfeed and a dedicated Slack channel. This helps create a feeling of alignment and encourages everyone to keep their goals up-to-date.

Goals feed

I can also see my most important initiatives as I plan my day, which constantly reminds me of the bigger picture and helps me align daily tasks to key initiatives.

If you don't want to use Friday, there are plenty of other goal-tracking tools with robust functionality. The only issue you will run into is the yet another tool problem. You will need to create your own habits and workflows to encourage your team to share progress.

Aisha's perspective

"Every month, everyone partakes in a monthly kickoff meeting, where we go over what we achieved the month prior and what we want to do for the upcoming month. We break down what we want Friday to accomplish, depending on different subjects, like the marketing side, or the product itself. We all set individual goals that we want to fulfill for the month.

We then see how these separate goals can come together so the team can reach an overarching goal of making Friday a product beneficial for companies.

The other places where I've worked didn't have these clear-cut goals that we addressed and had to achieve. There were tasks to be done, but nothing large enough to work toward every month.

I like the goal-setting feature we use because it helps me stay on track while also seeing the big picture. I know exactly where my progress is going and why I'm striving to reach the goal."

In conclusion

Staying aligned is not easy. If you focus on **roles** and **goals**, it will help significantly. It's okay to have meetings to talk it out, just make sure to write it all down and share it with others when you're done.

| 15 |

How to hold company meetups

One mistake people make when considering a work-from-anywhere model is assuming that meeting up in person is out of the question. Before the COVID-19 pandemic, every single leading remote-first company I can think of (i.e., Zapier, Automattic, GitLab, etc.) would meet up in the real world *at least once a year.*

That's because there is no replacement for face time.

As I've mentioned earlier in this book, you need to think about your communication and in-person interaction like tools in your toolbox. There is a time to meet in person, and there's a time to work from home. If you want to master WFA, you need to understand the value of company meetups and how to use them to build strong bonds with your team.

I've been to almost a dozen remote company offsites for numerous companies. I've also planned them. I've seen what works and what doesn't. My hope is that you can learn from the mistakes I've seen and made.

Why have an onsite?

The #1 reason why your company should meet up in person at least once a year is because it's the fastest way to recharge the "trust battery." If you want to accelerate and build better relationships and trust with your coworkers, the fastest way to do it is by spending quality time together.

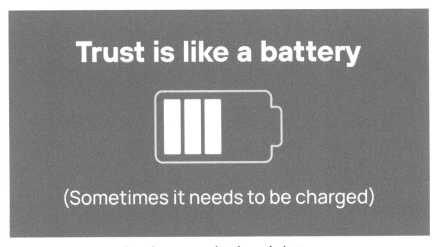

Sometimes you need to charge the battery

If building better relationships with your team is what you're optimizing for, you need to shape meetups to focus on this. I've been to meetups where we did heads-down work most of the time and it was an epic waste of time and money.

Company meetups is event planning!

Make no mistake - organizing company meetups is event planning. If you dislike event planning or believe it's not the best use of your time, it might be worth delegating to someone else on your team.

To illustrate, I worked for a 150-person company and an annual company meet-up consumed two people's time and attention for at least three months. At a smaller startup, we had a party planning committee handle the scheduling and coordination.

Even as a small startup, this can consume a meaningful amount of a founder's time and attention.

How often should meet-ups happen?

For early stage companies, you will feel a gravitational pull to hold a quarterly onsite, but I'd recommend against it for the following reasons:

- It's expensive
- A week-long meetup once a quarter is almost a month away from home every year
- You will spend too much time planning events and not enough time working on the business
- As you grow, you will have to scale back the frequency. It's inevitable.

I'd recommend early-stage companies have one or two meet-ups annually. If you need more face time with the team, I'd recommend having specific teams or individuals travel on their own.

For larger organizations, I'd recommend one meetup every year and to create loose guidelines around meeting up for collaboration, team building, and eating food together. For example, you could allocate a travel budget to a team that they can use at their own discretion.

Establish financial constraints

Speaking of budget, I'd encourage you to create guardrails when scheduling an onsite. You could have each person book their own travel and accommodations (easier to coordinate), but you will see a huge amount of variance if you don't create constraints. Some people on your team will book the cheapest flight possible, while others will book direct flights and spend twice as much money.

While you should expect some variance as people are flying in from different locations, you also need to apply constraints like:

- **A deadline** for when flights and accommodations should be booked

- **Costs that require leadership approval.** For example, if a flight costs over $1,000, you need to have someone approve it before booking

- **What costs can be expensed** – breakfast, lunch, and dinner? Or just lunch and dinner?

What should you do at a company meet-up?

These meet-ups should be focused on building better relationships and getting to know your team above all else. For example, you could:

- Eat lunch/dinner together (one of the best ways to get to know your team)
- Do an outdoor activity, like hiking or mini-golfing
- Go on a walking tour or visit a tourist destination

You don't need to overcomplicate this, especially if you are a small company. For example, at the first Friday meetup (we had 3 full-time employees at the time), I helped a coworker install siding on his house and hung out near the stream in his backyard.

I'm a little jealous..

If you're going to do work, I recommend tackling thorny problems that are best discussed in a face-to-face environment. For example, at another company meet-up for Friday, we discussed our company values and high-level strategy. Then, we took a boat ride. High-level brainstorming product brainstorming sessions work too!

What should the daily schedule look like?

I've experienced two different formats at organizations for which I've worked:

- Work in the morning, do team-building activities in the afternoon
- Work on specific days, and have dedicated team-building days

The right answer depends on the size of your business. If you are a larger business, I'd recommend grouping activities by the day because the coordination cost is lower. For a smaller startup, having variance throughout the day works.

The key to either of these approaches is to send an agenda before the events begin. People need to know what to expect and how they should prepare for the day. For larger companies, I'd recommend creating an agenda for the entire week and sharing it before everyone arrives.

Additionally, when meaningful discussion takes place, it needs to be documented in writing and shared with the broader group asynchronously. For example, if you hold break-out sessions with smaller teams, make sure to take notes and then share them with the broader group to ensure that the information is traveling across the organization.

What about drinking?

The answer to this question depends on the company you want to build. I've heard horror stories from peers about company meet-ups where people drink too much.

On one hand, you want to treat people like adults; but, on the other hand, you may not want things to get out of hand. So what do you do?

First, if someone wants to get their drink on, there's very little you can do about it. However, that doesn't mean you can't create constraints to set the tone. For example, one company where I worked would expense the first two drinks at a meal, but after that, the individual would need to buy their own drinks.

To be clear, this policy didn't stop certain individuals from drinking excessively, but it did create a cultural guardrail and set an expectation without being overly prescriptive.

Everyone is watching you

As a leader, your behavior at company meetups sets the tone. You should assume that someone on your team is always watching you. The behavior you exhibit when everyone meets up in person is much more likely to be remembered over the long term, as your in-person interactions are rare. This is your chance to shape and reinforce your company culture in a tangible way.

When the onsite ends...

After the onsite concludes, make sure to create a feedback loop to improve in the future. For example, you could send out an anonymous survey and ask questions like:

- On a scale of 0-10, would you recommend another company meetup?
- What is the reason for your choice?

In conclusion

People will remember your company meetups for years to come, so make them count! Optimize for getting to know your team above getting work done. You have the rest of the year to work.

| 16 |

How to hire from anywhere

Let's now talk about another key ingredient to growing your business from anywhere.

Hiring.

The promise of WFA means that you can hire amazing people, no matter where they live. The reality is that it can be tricky to identify and find talented people, especially if you are used to in-person interviews and trusting your gut.

In this chapter, I'm going to share everything I've learned about hiring people I've never met in person. As a frame of reference, we have teammates working across six different time zones at Friday spanning an 11-hour time difference. Most of the company has yet to meet each other in-person (yet).

How to get job applicants

If you want a decent number of applications for your job posting, there are a couple approaches you can take to open up the top of the funnel:

1. Post on a remote-first job board

WeWorkRemotely is the most well-known remote work job board I've found and is a great place to find quality applicants, especially for technical roles. You could also use hiring software like Workable to cross-post a listing across multiple job boards at once. Make sure the job posting is marked as remote-friendly though!

2. Post in multiple metros at once

Another hack I've seen (especially for fast-growing companies) is sharing the same job posting in several major cities *at the same time.* For example, you could post a remote-friendly software engineering role and mark the location as Boston. Then, you duplicate the same listing but change the location to New York or San Francisco.

There's a pool of potential candidates who may not be searching for a remote-first role, but may be open to it. Make sure to get in front of these people too!

Screening candidates

Remote-first roles tend to get a much higher volume of applications compared to job postings with geographical constraints, so you will need to aggressively filter as fast as possible.

How do you do this?

Only you know the right answer for your business, but the #1 factor I screen for (besides skill) is the ability to convey ideas and information in writing. At Friday, we do most of our work asynchronously, so we need to hire people who can communicate in writing.

1. Ask open-ended questions early

When someone completes an application for a job opening at Friday, we have them answer questions like:

- What's something you have built that you are super proud of and why?

- What's something you believe to be true that most people you know would disagree with you about?

- What would you like to be when you grow up?

These questions may seem random and bizarre, but they are intentionally mapped to our company values:

- *Question #1:* We like hiring people who love to learn and build new things (Our value is "always learning")

- *Question #2:* We aim to hire people with diverse perspectives, so we look for people who think outside the box and aren't afraid to share it.

- *Question #3:* We ask people what they want to be when they grow up to understand a bit more about what motivates them. This is also tied to our company value of not taking ourselves too seriously.

These questions create an immediate filter, especially for spam applications. It's hard to automate answers to these questions with a bot. You can also filter out individuals who aren't paying attention.

2. Ask for tangible samples of work

The next thing you want to screen for is someone's skills and ability. Have they created something that maps to what you are looking for in the role? If not, is there evidence that they can learn it?

For example, if you're trying to hire a writer, ask for writing samples. If you're trying to hire an engineer, ask for code samples or their GitHub profile. One of my favorite places to dig deeper is on the candidate's personal website or portfolio, if it exists. Typically, if something is on someone's personal website, it's of greatest importance to them. This can be work-related, a hobby, or something else.

3. You don't need to schedule a call right away!

Another trick I've learned is to use the open-ended responses to the questions as a conversation starter. I will send the candidate an email and say something like, "in your application you mentioned _____, do you mind sharing a bit more about this?"

Once again, I do this to assess someone's ability to write and convey ideas asynchronously. *I rarely jump on a video or phone call right away.* Sometimes I'll exchange a few emails with the candidate before we get on a call. Emails are cheap for both parties. Zoom calls are not.

I think I've found a great candidate. What do I do now?

It's not time to send an offer yet. There are still a couple more steps:

1. Schedule a video call

At this point, you should have 3-5 quality candidates. I'd encourage you to schedule time to chat over a video call. I typically ask more questions, share more about the role, expected responsibilities, and continue the conversation we started over email.

I recommend a video call so you can learn as much as possible about the person you're trying to hire. The bedrock for the conversation has been established through the email and work samples, so you're just looking for major red flags.

Depending on how the call goes, I'd strongly recommend the final and most important step in the interview process.

2. Work on a test project

For the final candidate(s), I recommend working on a *paid* test project that is limited in scope. Ideally, the project should take 3-6 hours. The basic criteria is below:

- **It should be paid** — This sends a signal that you value the candidate's time. I ask for their hourly contracting rate as a reference point

- **It should be limited in scope** — This test project can't be too time consuming, especially for candidates who are employed elsewhere

- **You should have a flexible timeline** — The candidate should be able to work on the project anytime they want, like weekends. Once again, we are testing someone's ability to work asynchronously

Think about it - if you are trying to figure out what it's like to work with someone full-time, what if you actually worked with them for a little bit? This is not rocket science.

A test project is a great way to reduce risk for both you and the candidate. The candidate can confirm that you are a nice person and you can figure out if the candidate is a good fit. I can't tell you how many times test projects have saved me from making a mistake hire.

I've found the person I want to hire!

Excellent! Now it's time to extend an offer. I recommend creating a job scorecard that outlines the role, responsibilities, and expected output.

1. Check references

It's easy to skip over references as it can introduce a coordination challenge, especially if you are hiring someone in another timezone. As a base case, I recommend sending questions over email and having the reference reply on their own schedule. It can't hurt to jump on a Zoom call too. The most important thing is to do the work and ping the references.

2. Logistical considerations

We use a professional employment organization (PEO) to handle paperwork and hiring across state boundaries (US-based). These vendors help you handle the complexities of dealing with each individual state and its local laws. While it's still annoying to deal with, a PEO does more of the work for you.

Likewise, if you hire internationally, you should explore a similar service so you can focus on growing your business instead of doing paperwork. There's a growing list of providers like Deel, Remote.com, Papaya Global, and other services worth looking into.

Aisha's perspective

"Getting hired at Friday was truly a special experience I won't forget. COVID-19 was still taking its toll on the world, so I knew there was a low chance of getting an in-person position. That meant that I could apply to places from all over, because the distance would not be an issue.

I stumbled across Friday's content marketing position and it intrigued me. I enjoy writing, but I never wrote on business and marketing. I decided to take a chance and emailed Luke my résumé and a few writing samples. The first ones I sent were all excerpts of my novels I'm writing. That wasn't a clear indication of if I could write for Friday. Then, I decided to send in some academic research papers in the hopes that my voice would be a bit more clear.

A week had passed and Luke mentioned that while it was clear that I could write, it wasn't enough to convince him that I could write about business topics. He decided to help me out and say what type of writing he was seeking, and proposed I write a short blog post about goal-setting if I wanted.

I vividly remember sitting at my dorm room's desk determined to write a blog post, something I had never written before. Four hours later, I had my first ever blog post written. I sent it to him not knowing what to expect, but it ended with a Zoom interview.

Because I already emailed Luke back and forth for a few days, the interview was short and more of a relaxed chat to get to know me and my goals. By the end of it, he gave me an offer.

It was a great learning experience for me, pushing me to places I never thought I'd have to go. I worked for this position, and it was great to see that it all paid off in the end."

In conclusion

Hiring people you have never met in person may seem scary, but if you create a process and stick by it, you can dramatically reduce the potential downside, which is all you can ask for when hiring. In the next chapter, we'll discuss how to onboard new hires, as sending the offer is only the beginning of the journey!

| 17 |

How to onboard a new hire from anywhere

After you hire someone, the next step is to onboard and bring them up to speed as quickly as possible. If you can refine your onboarding process to ramp someone in three months instead of six, that creates a massive efficiency boost for your business!

Like the previous chapter on hiring, I'm going to share high-level remote first tactics instead of sharing generic onboarding advice that you could find in another book.

Context is king

The most important thing you need to consider when onboarding new hires is that context is king. How have decisions been made in the past? What has the company learned over the past six months? What is rewarded? What are the quarterly goals for a team or department? How does the new hire's work fit into the bigger picture?

This information is all organizational context. Another word for this idea is tacit knowledge — it's the stuff that you learn over time that tends to be difficult to explain or document in writing.

I recommend abiding by the following principle: If you were to on-board a new hire tomorrow, how much could they learn and discover about the business before they need to meet with you?

If you have a ton of organizational context that is easily accessible, someone could learn on their own for days before they need to ping you. To be clear, I'm not advocating for ditching new hires. The goal is to make organizational context readily accessible instead of dripping it out through meetings. If you are the gatekeeper of this information, you will become a bottleneck and the new hire won't ramp as quickly as they could.

At Friday, when a new hire joins, they can access our software platform and see months of activity around goals, weekly updates, kudos, ice-breaker questions, and announcements. They don't need to rely on meetings or random interactions to learn this stuff.

New hire: day one

When someone new joins, make sure they complete the following ac-tivities on the first day:

1. Walk through the company handbook

Hold a meeting to walk through the company handbook and highlight company values, key goals, and other high-level principles. Make sure to ask if the new hire needs clarification on anything and make sure to share this information asynchronously so they can reference it later. Use their feedback to continue to iterate on your handbook and its con-tents.

2. Reinforce the key responsibilities and expected output

The next activity is to share a job scorecard that outlines what is expected from the new hire. *Specifically, what does success in the role look like?*

This can be a mixture of quantitative and qualitative data. This scorecard will most likely change over time, but you need a written artifact that the new hire and manager can stare at to understand if people are meeting or exceeding the requirements of the role.

To use a sports analogy, each player has a position on the field. While the team is expected to achieve a collective outcome (winning the game), each person needs a personal mission, like scoring points or preventing the opponent from scoring.

If a new hire doesn't know what position they need to play, they won't know if they are succeeding in the role. This is the purpose of the job scorecard. It creates clarity around individual performance and success. At a bare minimum, it helps you have richer conversations about these unspoken expectations.

3. Introduce to teammates ASAP

The next step is to connect the new hire to their teammates as quickly as possible. Do not assume that this will happen automatically. Some people will be extroverted and instantly ping others to chat, while others may feel nervous connecting with new people out of the blue.

4. Pair the new hire with an onboarding buddy

In addition to connecting the new hire with their immediate teammates, you should pair them with a dedicated onboarding buddy. The purpose of this buddy is to help acclimate the new hire to the company.

Ideally, this person is on an adjacent team vs. the immediate team. Here's why:

- A new hire may feel uncomfortable asking a "dumb" question as they are concerned about how they might be perceived by the rest of the group.

- The purpose of the onboarding buddy is to provide context about the company and how it works. Once again, context is king.

- It helps the new hire get to know someone on another team. Organizational silos form automatically, so you need to be constantly breaking them down.

5. Set up regular check-ins

Next, you need to create regular checkpoints for new hires. It's tough to ask for help as a new hire. It's even more difficult to ask for help when you are remote and don't have the random interactions to rely on. As a leader, *the responsibility is on you* to create regular check-ins to make sure roadblocks are removed as quickly as possible. Every roadblock extends the time it will take to fully ramp a new hire.

Synchronous check-ins

Throughout this book, we've talked about reducing time spent in meetings and holding Zoom calls for times when you want to build relationships, collaborate, or remove blockers.

When onboarding a new hire, I'd encourage you to default to video conversations most of the time (at least during the early stages of onboarding). This helps you get to know each other, it makes it easier to work through complex issues, and get on the same page. This is a time when you want to default to video calls!

Async check-ins

For many leaders, work can get overwhelming and you forget to sync up with a new hire as frequently as you wanted. That's why I encourage you to pair check-in meetings with an asynchronous check-in. We will discuss this strategy in more detail in the next chapter, but you should ask a few questions once a week (or two):

- How did you feel about the week?
- Do you have any blockers that we should discuss?
- Is there anything I can do to help you?

The answers to these questions should only be visible to you vs. the broader group.

Adjust your behavior over time

Another strategy is to adjust your behavior over time as the new hire becomes acclimated to the role and the day-to-day work. In the book, *High Output Management*, Andy Grove calls this idea "task-relevant maturity."

In short, you should manage differently depending on the level of experience someone has with a particular task. For example:

- When onboarding a new hire, you should be more hands-on and involved. By doing this, you speed up the pace of learning and help the employee onboard faster.

- For someone who has been working at your company for 10 years in the same role, they probably don't need supervision as they know what they are doing. Therefore, you can be hands-off.

For a new hire, I will often set up daily meetings for the first week as a way to help accelerate the pace of learning. For someone who's been working at the company for a few years, we may only need to meet a couple times a month.

Whenever I onboard a new employee, I will tell them that I am going to be more hands-on in the early days to help them onboard quickly, and that I will slowly back away over time. I find that setting this expectation provides clarity and helps me clarify that my goal is to help them onboard quickly vs. being a micromanager. ;)

Aisha's Perspective

"My onboarding experiences differ between the different positions I received over time. During my previous internships, my onboarding consisted of me receiving a checklist of my role and what I was expected to do during my time there. I remember there was a lot of paperwork to read. Then I was with all the other new hires while we went through the general overview of what to do and what not to do.

We then split up and went to our respective departments. I was taken to my desk and had a few online training courses to complete. Once I read all the information and was able to pass, I had my first meeting with my supervisor, where she introduced herself to me, went over my first tasks, and let me meet some people in my department.

My onboarding process at Friday was different because it was virtual. I was expecting a lot of PDF documents to review, but there was none of that. I was with one other intern, and Luke went through with introductions first, and then dove into the company handbook. I learned about Friday's mission and values. I was able to ask any questions or mention anything that stood out to me. It was quick and concise.

Afterward, I jumped right into a call with the entire team. We introduced ourselves, said our positions and presented a fun fact. That broke the ice immediately. After chatting for a while, we went over the goals we wanted to accomplish in the following month.

Overall, my onboarding experience with Friday was shockingly effective. There was no time wasted for paperwork or online training. I knew exactly what my role was and what I had to do. I also met the team all at once, instead of having to walk desk to desk and potentially distract them."

Final thought: discover what works for you

I'm going to let you in on a secret. Before the pandemic, many remote-first companies would encourage new hires to meet up in person with their manager as a way to accelerate onboarding. A new hire would fly to the city where the manager lived and hang out for the first week. While this may be impossible with a global team, it may be worth exploring as an option.

Think about it – if you can ramp up a new employee faster by meeting up in person during the early stages of onboarding, you could save tens of thousands of dollars in time cost. As a friendly reminder, the WFA movement is about picking the right tool for the task at hand. If hanging out in person accelerates onboarding, you should do it.

Friday Check-in

Hangout invite

12:30pm - 1:30pm

Share work and play some games together

✓ ✕

Company Goals

Details

Company Handbook

Role clarification

| 18 |

How to lead from anywhere

Now, let's talk about how to run a team from anywhere. Over the decades, countless books have been written on how to manage a team and be a great boss. Most of these books assume that the team is all together in the same location, which is clearly not the case these days.

In this chapter, I'm going to share specific tips and tactics when leading a distributed team. My hope is that you won't find generic "here's how you can be a good boss" advice in this chapter. We'll leave that stuff for the other books written 30 years ago.

What's different about managing a distributed team?

The first thing to consider is, "what makes leading a distributed team so difficult by default?"

I'd challenge the notion that it's tougher to lead when remote, but instead, that the tools you used in the office don't work as well now. It's like a carpenter using a hammer when they should be using a screwdriver instead. It's not that one tool is better than the other. It's that each tool serves a different purpose.

With that being said, leading a distributed team is not a walk in the park. Here are some challenges you will experience:

1. You can't manage by walking around

As I mentioned in the beginning of the book, the office provides a natural collision space for observing what's going on. You can use the office to "manage by walking around." As the name suggests, this activity is when you waltz around the office and talk to people. It gives you a chance to observe, nudge, and understand what's taking place. This activity gives you steady stream of data to improve your effectiveness.

When everyone isn't in the same room, you can't walk around and see what's going on. You may feel like you are flying blind. It's natural for leaders to try to replicate this office activity online by randomly pinging coworkers in workplace chat (management by chatting around), which can be annoying and distracting.

2. You aren't as persuasive

A hallmark trait of a great leader (at least the stereotype) is the ability to persuade and influence. Often this means you are great at talking in front of a group of people and can energize the room. When remote, you are much less persuasive because of the following reasons:

- **More of your communication is in writing** — this removes a lot of the emotion from communication. Being good at speaking and being effective at written communication are two different skills.
- **You don't have as great of a feedback loop** — Many leaders thrive on the feedback loop that exists in all-hands meetings and other group functions as it's easy to "read the room." Now, you try to be charismatic in a Zoom all-hands meeting only to be met by silence and blank stares from your team.

3. It's more difficult to understand how your team is feeling

Next up, it can be difficult to understand how someone on your team is feeling. When a team member walks into the office, you can often tell by the look on their face. As a leader, when you see that someone isn't feeling so well, you can intervene and try to help.

When remote, it takes much longer to discover that something is wrong, which means that it can take more time to resolve these potential problems.

4. It can be difficult to quantify output vs. activity

Leaders will rarely admit that they manage through "butts in seat," but it is easy to conflate activity with output. When remote, you can look at a workplace chat tool to see if people are online and equate this to "sitting at the desk, doing work." It can be easy to unintentionally grade people based on how quickly they reply to your messages and pings, even if that is not your intent.

5. You can't rely on meetings as much

Another reason why it's so difficult to lead a team when remote is that people become sick of the endless meetings. As a leader, meetings are a tool in your toolbox to create alignment, the feeling of connection, and to understand what's going on. But what happens if everyone is complaining about Zoom fatigue? Do you want to compound the issue even more?

What do you do?

If we look at the problems above, the root cause of remote management woes is that there's not enough data being exchanged between employees and leaders. The only way to fix this is by creating ways to speed up the flow of information between you and your team, but in a way that doesn't add another meeting or more distractions.

1. Run an asynchronous, routine check-in

The most important tip I have for leaders is to run a regular, asynchronous check-in. Every week (or two), ask your direct reports the following questions:

- How did you feel about the week? (emoji question)

- How productive were you this week? (1-10 scale)

- What went well this week? (open-ended)

- What was the worst part of your week? Anything I can do to help? (open-ended)

This is like a weekly update, but instead of being public and viewed by the entire team, it's only accessible to the employee and leader. This pulse check helps you understand how people are feeling about their week and also helps you kickstart more effective 1:1 meetings.

There's a few reasons why I recommend this approach:

- **People are more honest behind a screen** — according to internal research we've done with Friday users, at least 50% say they share more honest feedback using this async format than they do in a meeting. The responses give you a new level of insight, which helps kickstart better meetings.

- **The emoji question is powerful** — this may sound cheesy, but research shows that people process emojis in a similar way that they interpret facial reactions. If you want to really understand how people feel, ask them to respond with an emoji.

- **You can trend responses over time** — As a leader, you can look at the history of responses and see if things are trending in the right direction or not. This is much better than trusting your gut.

The insight from this routine will help you proactively identify potential problems and also help you discover ways to personalize someone's work experience. The output from this asynchronous routine is very similar to what you might learn in the first twenty minutes of a 1:1 meeting.

2. Spend time connecting in a 1:1 way

The second most important tool in your managerial toolbox is to have dedicated 1:1 conversations to get to know each person on your team. One of the most common examples is a 1:1 meeting.

I don't have *regularly* scheduled 1:1 meetings on my calendar. I will create on-demand 1:1s based on the feedback that I receive in the asynchronous check-in (see previous tip). Then, when I chat with someone, I try to spend extra time chatting with them as people instead of feeling pressure to check in on the status of a project.

If someone is struggling with work, I will find out through the check-in and will schedule a 1:1 meeting based on that. I find this process more effective as there are rarely awkward conversations. You always have something to talk about!

3. Have clear roles & expectations

This next tip applies to co-located teams, too; but as a leader, you need to create clarity of expectations and write them down. We discussed this idea in the chapter on hiring, but the premise is that you need role and goal clarity:

- **Role Clarity** — What is your area of ownership and focus? What is your position on the field?
- **Goal Clarity** — What projects, initiatives, or KPIs are you responsible for in the next month, quarter, or year?

4. Dedicate time to hang out

I'd strongly encourage you to dedicate time to collectively hang out as a team and do something besides work. We discussed this idea more in the chapter on how to feel connected.

For example, someone I know would hold Friday afternoon "happy hours" with his team. As the name suggests, the team would jump on a Zoom call early on a Friday afternoon and chat. While there would be a little bit of work discussion, the entire point of the call was to hang out. Many leaders have tried to do this throughout the pandemic, but often run into implementation problems, like:

- **Holding the event after regular work hours** — while it's possible that people may join after work, it's also a massive inconvenience. Respect the fact that people have lives outside of work
- **Not setting context** — set clear expectations around why the event exists and what people should expect when they show up. For example: "This event exists to hangout as a team. We won't discuss work or share status updates. Instead we will play games"

5. Don't be an information gatekeeper

It's easy for leaders to unintentionally hoard information. You may chat 1:1 with one person about a topic or goal and then have another conversation with someone else on your team. These discussions don't travel across the team, which means that the information is trapped and you are the only source. Congratulations, you are now a bottleneck!

Instead, you need to remove yourself as the bottleneck. The only way to do this is by documenting a conversation asynchronously and sharing the takeaways with the broader group.

6. Create and enforce communication norms

Speaking of communication, one area you will need to pay particular attention to is creating and enforcing communication norms. You are the communication architect for your team or company.

You don't need to go overboard, but gentle nudges and modeling the expected behavior goes a long way. For example, if you see a long discussion happening in Slack without a lot of progress being made, consider proposing that people jump on a video call instead.

If people are discussing something in a meeting that should be shared more broadly with the rest of the group, consider asking someone to take notes or record the Zoom call.

7. Avoid giving feedback asynchronously

Another pro-tip for leading a distributed team is to avoid giving negative feedback asynchronously. If you need to deliver bad news or feedback that could be interpreted in a variety of ways, make sure to do this in person, over a Zoom call, or on the phone.

At one of my first remote jobs, my boss delivered negative feedback to me over an email. I'm sure the intent was to be helpful, but it was scathing. I'm confident that if he shared the feedback over a video call, I would have interpreted it differently. Written messages can be interpreted in many ways, so you need to tap into the fast feedback loop that a real-time conversation enables.

Side note — if a software vendor offers the ability to share performance feedback through software, you should run the other way. It's a terrible practice that will cause issues at some point.

In conclusion

To wrap up this chapter, effectively managing a distributed team is not too different from the best practices you've seen in management books written decades ago. The major differences are that you need to over-index on building relationships and to act like a communication architect to make sure information flows where it should.

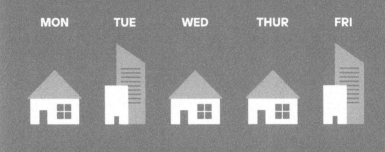

MON   TUE   WED   THUR   FRI

| 19 |

What about hybrid work?

As a byproduct of the pandemic, many companies have decided to implement a hybrid approach where people work from home a couple days a week, with the option to visit the office 1-2 days/week for collaborative activities, team bonding, and meetings. In fact, this mode of work may be the "new normal."

On the surface, this makes a ton of sense and fits neatly into the work-from-anywhere framework proposed earlier in the book. In reality, there's some hidden complexity you will need to deal with that you may be underestimating right now.

In this chapter, I'm going to discuss the benefits and pitfalls of hybrid work. Similar to working remotely, many forward-thinking companies were already offering this work model before the pandemic started, so we don't need to reinvent the wheel.

The gravitational pull to hybrid

The rationale behind a hybrid work environment is straightforward. Working from home has benefits, like being able to focus and do deep work without distractions. Working from an office has benefits, like watercooler discussion and the ability to grab lunch with coworkers on a whim.

Some people on your team would prefer to work from home a few days a week, while others would like to work from the office every day of the week. Another group would love to ditch the office completely and live a thousand miles away from the HQ.

As a company, what do you do? Different people have different preferences. If you are too opinionated, you could alienate a portion of your company, which may cause employee turnover. If you don't have an opinion, you might inadvertently create chaos.

What are your options?

Contrary to what you might read online, there are many flavors of hybrid that you can pursue.

- You can be fully remote, but encourage people to meet up in person when it makes sense (like offering to pay for a group lunch)

- If you have enough density of talent in a particular city, you could pay for co-working space for the team

- You could keep your office space, but create a rigid policy around meeting up in person, (i.e., only meet up for high-level brainstorming, team lunches, and quarterly performance conversations).

- You could expense co-working space for individuals who need to get out of the house

- You could encourage team leaders to use their best judgement and push down the decision to them.

Which format should you decide?

First of all, there is no perfect solution. Whatever decision you make will have advantages and disadvantages. You need to focus on maximizing the upside (both for the business and the employee), while reducing the potential downside.

So how might you make this decision?

1. Think about talent

As a starting point, you need to think about the existing team and potential future hires. If you return to the office (even a few days a week), will this decision limit the pool of talent you can hire? If you force employees to come back to the office for a couple days a week, you are creating a geographical constraint as *your team will still need to commute to the office.*

2. Talk to your team

Consider running a survey or holding small focus groups to understand where your team falls. It's possible that the right answer will become obvious in the data, but don't be surprised if 60% want a hybrid work environment, 20% want fully remote, and another 20% want to return to the office. You should expect the survey responses to follow a standard distribution curve.

3. Have an opinion

At the end of the day, you need to take a stance and make it known to the rest of the company, ideally in writing. *There is no perfect solution.* If you wait too long, people on your team will leave because of your indecision. Some of your employees may consider moving elsewhere, but they are waiting for you to make up your mind.

Issues with hybrid work

If you decide to pursue a hybrid model, there are a few potential issues that you should try to avoid.

1. You need to be intentional about sharing information

As you meet and collaborate in the real-world, you will build up institutional knowledge inside your team that will not magically flow to the remainder of the company unless you regularly document the highlights of your conversation and share it with others, asynchronously.

This may feel like extra work to you. You are right! It's not easy to change habits. This is why many remote-first companies are not fans of hybrid work arrangements. If you don't create a habit, some members of your team will feel disconnected and out of the loop as you've created an uneven playing field.

2. Cliques will form if you aren't careful

Next up, in a hybrid work environment, certain relationships between coworkers will deepen, while others will not. For example, if you only meet up with immediate team members in person, you will naturally get to know them vs. people on other teams. This can create an "us vs. them" mentality. In psychology, this is known as the in-group vs. the out-group.

While this dynamic is unavoidable at work (as you will always spend more time with immediate team members compared to people in other departments), if you aren't intentional, you could create a toxic environment without even trying.

To illustrate, at a company for which I used to work, employees were given flexibility around when they could go into the office. One group would visit on specific days of the week. Relationships strengthened for this team at the expense of their coworkers. Other people would show up to the office and were not invited to lunch. In short, this team acted like they were the only ones in the office, which caused tension.

3. You will still need to make difficult decisions

At the end of the day, if you think a hybrid work environment is a path to avoid making tough decisions for your company, you will be disappointed. You will still need to create high-level policies, coordinate desks, and a lot more. In fact, you will need to do more coordination than if you made a decision to go fully remote or 100% back to the office.

For example, I worked at a company where every employee (even if they were in the office) needed to join video calls on their own computer instead of using a shared webcam in a conference room. This policy was an effort to include remote employees as first-class citizens. We should expect hybrid organizations will need to create their own operating procedures in a similar fashion, which takes work!

4. Relying on in-person discussion can become a crutch

Another pitfall I've experienced working inside a hybrid organization is that there's a tendency to delay important conversations until you meet in person. For example, I worked at a company that had an annual company onsite. Two months before the company onsite happened, teams would create placeholders for future discussion and would say, "we should discuss this topic at the meet-up."

This was a terribly unproductive approach. Day-to-day work ground to a halt for at least a month; and while the company meet-up was amazing, punting decisions created an enormous bottleneck.

The WFA movement is about freeing up each person to run at their own pace. If you need to meet in person to make an important decision, you are creating roadblocks that will slow your company down.

4. You can't work every day from the office

As a leader, you will need to be intentional about how much time you spend in the office. You may need to force yourself to work from home. If the leadership team works out of the office five days a week, this behavior lays a foundation for the rest of the company, especially those who want more responsibility or a promotion. Basically, if someone wants to be promoted, they need to come into the office everyday to make sure that the leadership team sees them. This phenomenon is known as the mere exposure effect. People develop a preference for something after repeated interactions. If you aren't careful, you can create a toxic work environment.

5. You need to create a level playing field in meetings

Finally, it's easy to create an uneven playing field in meetings. Imagine a hybrid meeting with group of people in a conference room and a few people joining remotely. The group in the conference room may forget about the remote team members as they are "out of sight, out of mind". The conversation amongst those in the same location is much faster-paced and richer. The people joining remotely don't have nearly as much of a signal and it can be tricky to keep up. This dynamic makes it difficult for the remote team members to participate. The remote team members have a handicap compared to those in the office.

I first ran into this problem almost five years ago at a previous employer. The CEO forced everyone to join meetings via Zoom, even for those were working out of the office. At first, I thought this was a terrible idea, but after time, I realized that it was brilliant. By putting everyone on a level playing field, you can have much more thoughtful meetings where everyone is encouraged to participate.

How we work at Friday

I think it's helpful to share how we work at Friday to help illustrate some of these points. I've decided that I want to hire the best people I could find, regardless of location. As a result, our team is scattered across six time zones. I will always optimize for finding talented people over location. That's the most important factor.

With that being said, we have clustered US-based hires around two cities: - Portland, Maine, and Nashville, Tennessee. If I can find someone in one of these cities, I will happily make the hire.

Even though we have grouped our US-based hiring in two cities, we are still an all-remote company. I work from home every day, even though I live 20 minutes away from a few of my coworkers. We will try to meet in-person periodically, but it's something that happens once in a while instead of every week.

In short, I consider being able to meet up in person regularly as a nice to have, not a must have.

In conclusion

At Friday, the primary goal of meeting up in person is to hang out, grab lunch, and enjoy each other's company. If you pursue a hybrid work model, I'd encourage you to adopt a similar mindset.

If you try to introduce too much complexity, it will distract you from growing your business and will create problems. There is no perfect solution: talk to your team, experiment, and make changes as you learn.

Finally, the gauntlet of productivity.

| 20 |

How to stay productive and avoid burnout

I recently had a conversation with someone who was new to remote work. I asked him what his biggest personal struggle was. He replied:

> "I have so much more free time because I don't have to commute anymore, but I waste so much time, so I finish my day wondering what I even accomplished."

This statement perfectly describes Parkinson's Law, which says: "*work expands to fill the time available for its completion.*" If you give yourself a lot of time to accomplish a task, you will procrastinate and wait as long as possible to do the work.

If you think about it, you have probably spent most of your life in environments where structure was created for you. As a child, you had to be at the bus stop at a specific time to make sure you made it to school on time. Your school day was already planned for you. You would need to rotate from room to room every hour. At the end of the day, you would take the bus home. Rinse and repeat.

In a work-from-anywhere environment, the lack of structure creates a feeling of newfound freedom, but it can also be overwhelming. Every day feels the same. You work where you live. You start working too early, end up spending too much time browsing Reddit, and end your day scrambling to get work done.

I've felt this, too. In the remainder of the chapter, I'm going to share how you can be productive and stop burning out.

Create structure & definition

The first and most important problem to solve is that you need to create structure to your day. You can't rely on the commute to the office to help you ease into your work. You also don't have observable signals at the office that encourage you to finish up your work and go home at a reasonable hour.

Create start and end times for your day

An easy way to create definition to your day is by reviewing your meetings and seeing when you could start and end the day. Reflect and write down when you are most productive and when you lose focus.

For example, I start my day at 8 a.m. and end at 4 p.m. most days. I know I'm most productive in the morning and least productive in the afternoon. I use my daily planner in Friday to quickly review my day and then use the data to see when I'm most productive.

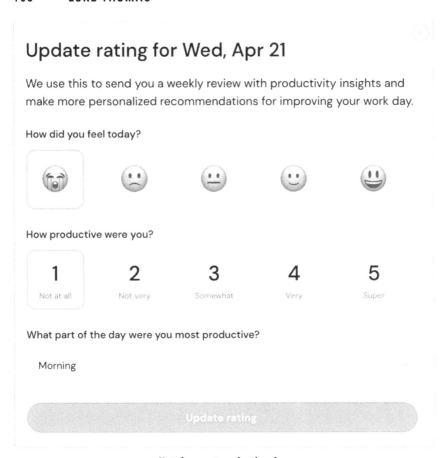

Not the most productive day.

Then, I will update my Friday profile to share the hours when I normally work. I will also update my Slack account to go into do-not-disturb outside of my normal working hours. This helps reduce notifications outside of my workday.

Notification schedule

You'll only receive notifications in the hours you choose. Outside of those times, notifications will be paused. Learn more

Allow notifications:

| Weekdays ⌄ | 08:00 ⌄ | to | 16:00 ⌄ |

You won't receive notifications on Saturday or Sunday.

An easy win in Slack

As a leader, your behavior sets the tone for others. If you don't model this behavior, people will follow your lead and replicate what you do. If you ping people on the weekend in Slack, others will assume that they can do the same.

Force yourself to move, everyday

I'm sure you already know that physical exercise is beneficial for the mind and body. You don't need to run a marathon before work starts, but you need to find time to move every day. It's so easy to forget about this when you work where you live. There's a gravitational pull to stay home and you must resist it.

Start a fitness routine with coworkers. Keep a fitness journal. Download a habit tracker app. Find ways to reward yourself. If you aren't getting some amount of physical activity everyday, you aren't doing your best work. It's just that simple.

Be intentional about how you allocate your time and attention

Another tip is to find better ways to allocate your time and attention. Consider blocking off time on your calendar to focus, use a Pomodoro timer, or listen to focus music (I recommend Brain.fm). For example,

I use the Friday chrome extension to block social media websites and mute Slack notifications so I can stay focused.

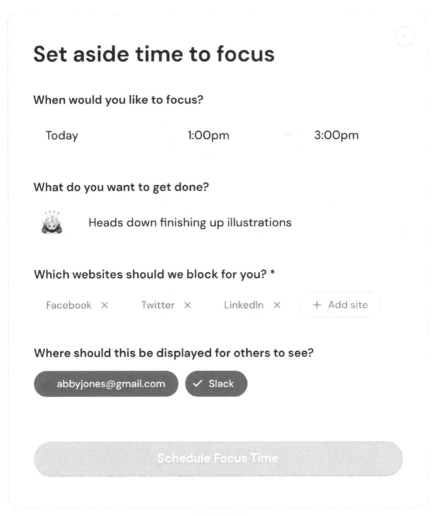

Block it all!

Feeling unproductive? Change your environment

When I'm feeling unproductive, I force myself to relocate to another location. I could move to another part of my house, or go to the local coffee shop, but the key is to change my environment to reset my brain.

Create work habits

Another tip is to create habits of planning and reflection. Create checkpoints to prioritize your work, and when the work is complete, reflect and think about what you can do to improve in the future.

For example, every day before I start work, I ask myself a few questions:

- How are you feeling?
- What are your must wins for today?
- What's on your mind?

I've done this exercise for years and find that it helps me establish a habit of doing intentional work.

Aisha's Perspective

"When I first started working remotely, I didn't know how to feel. On one hand, I didn't have to plan my day expecting to commute. That meant I could save time between going to classes and doing other activities. Because I was no longer in the office, there was no one to check up on me to make sure I got my tasks done at a certain time.

The fear of procrastination crept up a couple of times. I told myself that I'd do the work eventually, because I had so much time to do it. Or it was the other way around, where I did the work instantly, and then struggled to figure out what to do with my free time.

Working at Friday, I knew I needed to have a clear idea of how to tackle my work day. Without classes to force me onto a schedule, I had to come up with my own. My routine goes a little something like this:

I wake up and eat some breakfast. During this, I check my email to see if anyone messaged me. Then I check my workplace chat app to see team updates.

I do my daily standup, where I force myself to think about what I have to do for the day. Sometimes I'm able to do them all in a day, other days I can't. This is just something to guide me.

If I have any meetings, I jump on the Zoom calls to connect with my coworkers.

At around noon, I take a lunch break. Sometimes I walk to a cafe nearby to clear my head.

After my break, I power through the last few hours of work, thinking of what I can finish and what I may have to do tomorrow.

After work I usually go do some physical activity, whether it's going to the gym, doing a spin class, or just running along a trail.

This is just a basic routine I use. To help me focus during work, I usually put on a music playlist where I can measure my time spent doing that task.

Some tips I would give to people new to working remotely:

1. Don't force a schedule. The point of having a flexible schedule is that it can be flexible. Having something too rigid could lead to burnout.

2. Take breaks. Even if it's just standing up to get a glass of water, it can help for sure.

3. Space out your work. Doing things all at once can only last you so long.

4. Partake in icebreakers and communicate with your team. Learning about coworkers and speaking with them face to face is a nice change of pace from just working nonstop 24/7."

The little things add up

One final point. Pay attention to the small details that help drive moments of productivity. For example, I know that if I stand at my desk or listen to focus music with my noise-cancelling headphones, it will increase my chances of doing deep work. I'm sure you have your own triggers, too, just make sure you pay attention to the little cues.

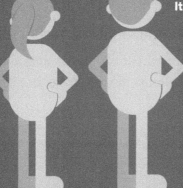

| 21 |

12 Mental models for success

In this chapter, I'm going to share 12 mental models for working from anywhere. Think of this chapter as a collection of key principles that were scattered throughout the book.

If you don't know what mental models are, it's a short and memorable phrase used to describe a concept, framework, or worldview that you keep in your mind.

1. Remote work isn't about working from home

The work-from-anywhere movement isn't about working from home. It's not only about *where* you decide to work from, but it's about *when* you work.

The power of this shift allows you to better integrate work and life. It also allows the company to tap into when each person is most productive, which means this shift is good for the business and the employee!

2. If it doesn't persist, it doesn't exist

When working from anywhere, if something is not documented, you should act like it doesn't exist. This applies to meetings, tasks, goals/OKRs, and more.

Written artifacts (or video recordings) provide context, and this context helps everyone understand what each other is working on. Every piece of context adds another block to the foundation of your organization.

3. Communication pumps keep information flowing

Think of workplace communication like a plumber thinks about plumbing. You need pipes to make sure that water can travel from one location to another. But you also need pumps to regulate the flow.

Now substitute water for information.

If you roll out workplace chat software, Zoom, and other communication tools, you have laid the pipes for better communication, but it lacks rules and logic to create predictability. Like a water pump, you need a system that helps information flow, with as little human effort as possible.

You can use software like Friday to help automate weekly updates, daily standups, and other recurring communication, which creates a predictable flow of information and keeps everyone in the loop.

4. Communication pipes come in different types

Back to the plumber. The plumber knows that certain pipes are best for a particular job. Similarly, you need to pick the best communication tool or channel for the task at hand.

As the communication theorist Marshall McLuhan once said, *"The medium is the message."* The communication channel you use shapes the way your message is interpreted. Instead of spending so much time thinking about the perfect thing to say in a meeting, consider the channel and tool you use to deliver the message.

5. Poor visibility is a liability

As Andy Grove said in his book, *High Output Management:*

> "Information-gathering is the basis of all other managerial work, which is why I choose to spend so much of my day doing it."

As you work in different locations, it's natural to feel disconnected from what your team is working on and how they are feeling. This lack of visibility creates a growing liability that you will need to address.

You need to confront this problem and develop ways to understand what people are working on, and how they are feeling about their work. Ideally, this doesn't require spending your day sitting in meetings.

6. Your coworkers can't feel like robots

When you work with people in different locations and spend most of your day communicating from behind a screen, it's easy to feel like your coworkers are robots, not people. After all, most of the time they're just a tiny little avatar on a screen.

If you plan on building healthy long-term working relationships, you need to constantly remind yourself that your coworkers have hobbies, interests, and career aspirations. The minute you feel your coworkers are emotionless robots is the minute your workplace relationships will start to deteriorate.

7. Clock results, not hours

When running a company from anywhere, it becomes difficult to understand what people are doing at every moment during the day. In fact, it's impossible, so you may as well stop trying. The days of managing by walking around are over. In the industrial age, when someone wasn't working on the factory floor, work wasn't getting done. But things have changed. Inspiration can strike anywhere, anytime.

If you want to adapt, you will need to create clarity around the expected output of individuals, teams, and departments.

- **Role clarity** — What are the key outputs of the role?
- **Goal clarity** — What do you aim to accomplish in the next week or month?

8. Process makes perfect

If you want a predictable outcome, you need a process for achieving the goal. If you want to make great hires, you need a process. If you want to onboard people quickly and with less stress, you need a process. If you want to become a great manager and understand what's going on at work, you need a process.

If you have a process, but it's not written down, you don't have a process (see mental model #2).

9. You can change everything, except time zones

Many parts of your business can be changed. You can hire new people, create new processes, change your pricing, and you can roll out new software. But the one thing you can't change is time zone differences. If you hire someone six time zones away, there's nothing you can do to change this reality.

Therefore, if you're new to running a business from anywhere, consider the amount of time zone overlap that exists in your company. Save yourself some trouble in the early days and constrain time zones. It will save you pain as you get up to speed.

10. Have fewer, better meetings

Many internal meetings could have been an email. Meetings are best for building better relationships, collaborating around a complex topic, and removing blockers.

If you spend most of your time conveying information in meetings, consider ditching the meeting and sharing the information asynchronously instead.

11. Take personal responsibility

Working from anywhere is founded on the premise that employees are adults and should be treated that way. With that being said, this is a reciprocal relationship that requires that everyone take personal responsibility.

Working from anywhere is not perfect and problems will pop up. Instead of waiting for the business to create a policy to "fix" the situation, people should proactively come up with potential solutions *on their own*. Oftentimes, the pain someone experiences when remote are personal pain points, not team or company-wide pain points.

Each person's work experience is suspect to variance, so each person needs to feel empowered to improve their own situation without making a broad-brush policy change.

12. Get out of the house

You aren't supposed to spend every moment of your life at home. Social interaction is important, but you won't find it if you act like a hermit. Volunteer in your community. Find people with shared interests. Learn a new hobby. Get out of the house!

It's true that remote work can be more isolating by default, which is why you need to take the initiative. Maybe it's time to get to know your neighbors?

| 22 |

Our favorite software

In this final chapter, we'll share our favorite software and tool recommendations to help you work-from-anywhere. We'll break this section down into three parts; for you, your team, and for your company.

Try Friday?

We'd love it if you gave Friday.app a try. We've created a command center for working from anywhere.

For individuals, we can help you roadmap your day, stay focused, block distractions, and do your best work. For teams and organizations, we can help you stay in sync with fewer meetings and see what's going on at work. Long story short, we've created a home for the most important stuff at work that complements workplace chat tools like Slack and Microsoft Teams.

For you

Here are my favorite tools for personal productivity.

1. Brain.fm

Brain.fm is an audio service to help you focus, relax, sleep, and meditate. I'm a huge fan of this service as it forces me to focus. The team at Brain.fm has spent years researching the science of how to become more productive through audio. As an alternative, you can find focus music on Youtube or Spotify.

Cost: $49/year

2. Krisp.ai

Krisp is software that helps you mute background noise.It helps you make sure you never have to worry about your environment when you take a call. With Krisp, you can easily jump on Zoom from a noisy coffee shop or co-working space, which makes life so much better for the audience. It's especially great if you work from home and your dog randomly barks.

Cost: $60/year

3. Cleanshot for Mac

Cleanshot is the easiest way to quickly take screenshots or record gifs from your Mac computer and share them with others. I love this app because I tend to share screenshots quite a bit throughout the day. If you use a PC, try CloudApp or Skitch.

Cost: $29

For your team

Now, we'll share our favorite software picks for your team. Most of these products offer a free plan so you can try before you buy.

1. Slack

Every distributed team should consider using workplace chat and Slack (despite its flaws) is our pick here. When used within reason, Slack is a great place to have quick back-and-forth conversations with your team. If you use the Microsoft suite, you might consider using Teams. Another alternative is Glip by RingCentral, which neatly bundles chat, phone, and meetings together.

Cost: $80/year

2. Zoom

For video chat, Zoom is the most reliable service we've found. There's a reason why it was so quickly adopted when everyone started working from home at the beginning of COVID. Zoom also offers a generous free tier.

Cost: $149/year

3. Trello

There are so many project management tools you could choose from, but we like Trello. It's a simple and easy way to store and collaborate on projects, especially for non-technical teams.

Cost: $120/year

4. Loom

Loom is an easy way to share quick asynchronous video with others. It's perfect for situations when you need to share context, but don't want to hold a meeting. I use Loom for product/UX feedback and to create context outside of a meeting.

Cost: $96/year

5. Grain

Grain.co is an easy way to record and quickly share video clips of your Zoom meetings with your team. This is perfect for customer conversations where you'd like to share interesting snippets from a meeting.

Cost: $144/year

6. Butter

Butter.us is a fun way to have interactive, virtual workshops with your team. The experience is much more fun than Zoom, which means that it boosts participation from your team. If you do team building, happy hours, or other internal calls, you should use Butter for them.

Cost: free (paid plan coming soon)

7. Almanac

Almanac.io is a team wiki for structured documentation, like your company handbook or other policies. It also offers the ability to version your documents and create a digital trace of how a particular document changes over time. As an alternative, you might consider using Notion, Google Docs, or Microsoft Word.

Cost: $1200/year+

Tools for running your company

Finally, here's the software and tools I recommend for running a company from anywhere.

1. Post Scan Mail

If you don't have an office, I'd strongly recommend using a virtual mailbox provider to handle your business mail instead of your home address. Post Scan Mail (or another provider like Virtual Post Mail or Earth Class Mail) will receive your mail and process it digitally, so you can disconnect your business address from your home. This is especially important if you plan on moving soon or would like to travel to another location for part of the year.

Cost: $180/year+

2. OpenPhone

On a similar note, I'd strongly recommend that you set up a dedicated business phone, especially if you are an early stage startup. If you give out your cell phone, you will get random calls and messages for years to come. That's why I recommend OpenPhone. OpenPhone makes it easy to forward and handle phone calls and texts, so you can keep your cell phone number for family and friends.

Cost: $120/year

3. Deel

If you plan on hiring full-time employees or contractors outside the US, I recommend using Deel to handle payments and compliance. This has been a game-changer for my company. It saves me a ton of time and helps me sleep better at night, too!

Cost: $420/year+

4. Rippling

Next up, you should use Rippling to handle your HR and IT needs, especially for team members based in the United States. It offers a PEO, which allows you to outsource annoying compliance issues as you hire full-time employees from multiple states. It also offers other features, like an applicant tracking system and time tracking. Rippling helps you handle the people side of the business.

Cost: $96/year+

5. 1Password

Make sure you don't forget about keeping your data safe when working from anywhere. That's why I recommend using a password manager like 1Password to generate secure passwords and to securely share this information with other members of your team.

Cost: $48/year

In conclusion

You should expect to see more tools and products emerge as working from anywhere continues to grow in popularity. We hope these recommendations restore your sanity and help you stay in sync with your team.

.

FEEDBACK

If you have feedback or would like to chat about something covered in this book, please reach out:

- **Email:** luke@friday.app
- **Text:** (629) 240-2263

You can read the online version of this book and access a free audio book (plus other downloadable content) at: **www.friday.app/anywhere**. We plan on releasing video tutorials to supplement the content discussed in this book.

If you enjoyed this book, do you mind leaving a positive review on Amazon? We'd greatly appreciate it!

CPSIA information can be obtained
at www.ICGtesting.com
Printed in the USA
LVHW071544150721
692783LV00012B/341

9 781087 874241